American Inside Out Evolution

Teacher's book

Beginner

SUE KAY
VAUGHAN JONES

macmillan education

Macmillan Education

Companies and representatives throughout the world
American Inside Out Evolution. Teacher's Edition Beginner

Sue Kay and Vaughan Jones
Written by Helena Gomm
Adapted by Simon Campbell, George Wells and Catherine Gray / Part of the writing team from The Content Station

Published under licence from Macmillan Publishers Ltd.
Macmillan is a registered trademark.
First edition published 2017

ISBN: 978-607-473-613-7

Based on New American Inside Out Teacher's Edition Beginner
D.R. © Macmillan Publishers, S.A. de C.V. 2008
Published under license from Macmillan Publishers Ltd.

Editorial Manager: Patricia Muradas
Editorial Operations Coordinator: Veronica Teodorov Ferreira
Editor: Cintia Zaitune
Concept design: Martha Tadaieski
Page make-up: The Content Station
Graphic Production: Kelly Gobbo
Photographic research: The Content Station
Cover concept and design: Jean Aranha
Cover photo: Giovanni Gagliardi | Dreamstime

We are grateful for permission to reprint the following copyright material: Page iv: Quotation from Language and Problems of Knowledge by Noam Chomsky copyright © Noam Chomsky 1988 Massachusetts Institute of Technology, reprinted by permission of The MIT Press, Cambridge, Massachusetts. Page iv: Quotation - Reproduced by permission of Oxford University Press. From Oxford Applied Linguistics: Understanding Second Language Acquisition by Rod Ellis © Rod Ellis 1985. New Edition OAL: A Study of Second Language Acquisition published 2008.

CANIEM No. 2275

Macmillan Publishers S.A. de C.V.
Insurgentes Sur 1886
Col. Florida, CP 01030
Álvaro Obregón
Ciudad de México
Tel: +52 (55) 5482 2200
elt@grupomacmillan.com

www.grupomacmillan.com
www.macmillan.com.mx
www.macmillanenglish.com

Printed in Brazil

This book was printed in October, 2017 by: Eskenazi Indústria Gráfica Ltda, Avenida Miguel Frias Vasconcelos, 1023 - Jaguaré - São Paulo - SP.

Contents

Student's Book Content Map

	Units and topics	Speaking and Writing	Reading and Listening	Grammar, Vocabulary, and Pronunciation
Page 8	0 Instructions **Classroom**	Activities to introduce classroom language including teacher and textbook instructions		
Page 10	1 ID **Names and numbers** **Everyday objects**	S Exchanging names and numbers S Identifying everyday objects WB W Punctuation (question mark/period) Writing short questions and answers	L James Bond L What's in your bag? **Language for Life:** Personal Information **Life Skills** Studying: Materials	G *my/ your/ his/ her.* Singular and plural nouns. *this/these* V Names. Numbers 1-10. Everyday Objects P Alphabet. Vowel Sounds
Page 16	2 International **Countries** **Nationalities** **Prices**	S Saying where you are from S Talking about prices	L Rock star talent L Prices around the world **Language for Life**: In a store **Life Skills** Cultural Awareness: Food and Celebrations	G *be*: simple present Prepositions: *in/near* *How much ...?* V Countries. Nationalities. Numbers 11–199. Prices P Word stress: numbers
Page 22	3 Family **Family** **Introductions**	S Talking about your family W Someone in your family	L My family (1) L My family (2) R Famous families **Language for Life**: Introductions **Life Skills** Communication: Showing Interest	G *How old ...?* Possessive *'s/s'. our/ their. have/ has* V Family P *an* + vowel / *a* + consonant
Page 28	Review A	Pages 28, 29: **Grammar / Vocabulary / Pronunciation review** Pages 30, 31: **Reading and Listening, Writing (form filling) & Speaking**		

Introduction

In ***American Inside Out Evolution***, meaning is central to everything we ask the students to do. Instead of basing lessons on invented people in imaginary situations, we present target language in real contexts and authentic texts. We believe that the richest "source of meaning" in any lesson is what each student brings into the classroom-their thoughts, ideas, opinions, experiences and feelings. Our materials are therefore designed to help the teacher exploit this resource and make important and memorable connections between the target language and the students' own lives.

In addition to this fundamental core principle, here are three more important beliefs that have guided us in our teaching and writing over the years:

Sue Kay and *Vaughan Jones*

- Vocabulary should share center stage with grammar. Words are the basic building blocks of any language.
- Language skills are best acquired through lots of practice. You learn to read by reading; you learn to speak by speaking, etc. Attempts to identify and then practice discrete sub-skills are not convincing.
- There can never be enough practice activities!

Engaging content

The American linguist and philosopher Noam Chomsky once said:
"The truth of the matter is that about 99% of teaching is making the students feel interested in the material. Then the other 1% has to do with your methods."

While we might want to quibble with the percentages, we would nevertheless agree whole-heartedly with the central message in Professor Chomsky's assertion: namely, students learn best when they're interested in the material. It's as simple as that. A text might contain six beautifully crafted examples of the simple past, a good spread of high frequency lexical items, and exemplify some useful functional language, but if it doesn't engage the students, if they can't relate to it, if it feels alien to them, then the most important ingredient for successful learning is missing.

In *American Inside Out Evolution*, we've drawn on our own classroom experience, and that of our colleagues around the world, to select topics, texts, and tasks that engage students both emotionally and intellectually. Students are our richest resource. They come to class with their own knowledge of the world, their own tastes, feelings, and opinions. It's up to us to exploit this rich resource by organizing learning around topics that they can relate to—topics that are part of their life experience.

Structured support

We all know that learning a language is a messy, non-linear business. We're dismayed when there seems to be little correlation between what is taught and what is learned! However, there is plenty of evidence to suggest that "instructed" learners (those who attend classes or follow a course of study) learn faster, and ultimately attain a higher level of proficiency than "non-instructed" learners.

In *American Inside Out Evolution*, new language input is carefully controlled: we aim to maximize exposure to high frequency language appropriate to this level. Students are encouraged to notice new grammar and new vocabulary in contexts where the meaning is clear. They are then given opportunities to manipulate the new language and try it out in different situations. They discover why using one particular form rather than another one actually matters: not just because it's right or wrong, but because it does or doesn't communicate a meaning successfully. The emphasis is always on what students can do with the language rather than what they know about the language. The new language is systematically reviewed and recycled until finally the students feel confident enough to use it to make their own meanings. It becomes part of their available repertoire. It has been "learned."

Real world tasks

We're strong believers in the old adage: "practice makes perfect." *American Inside Out Evolution* emphasizes output, particularly speaking, and there are a huge number of tasks that are designed to develop fluency. Students practice functional language in sections entitled *Language for Life*. But for the most part, the speaking tasks simply encourage the students to talk about things that actually matter to them, rather than playing roles or exchanging invented information. One of our main objectives is to ensure that the language our students spend time rehearsing in the classroom is transferable to the real world. By orchestrating tasks that require the students to use grammar and vocabulary to make meaningful utterances, this objective becomes obtainable. As the linguist and academic Rod Ellis reminds us:

"It is the need to get meanings across and the pleasure experienced when this is achieved that motivates second language acquisition."

www.insideout.net
"the art of communication"

Components of the course

Student's Components

Student's Book with access code to Digital Student's Book
see pages vi-ix

Workbook with access code to Digital Workbook
see page ix

Companion website: www.macmillan.com.br/americaninsideoutevolution

- Free app

Teacher's Components

- Teacher's Edition with access code to Teacher's Presentation Kit with Extra Resources
- Test Generator
- Class audio CDs
- Companion website: www.macmillan.com.br/americaninsideoutevolution

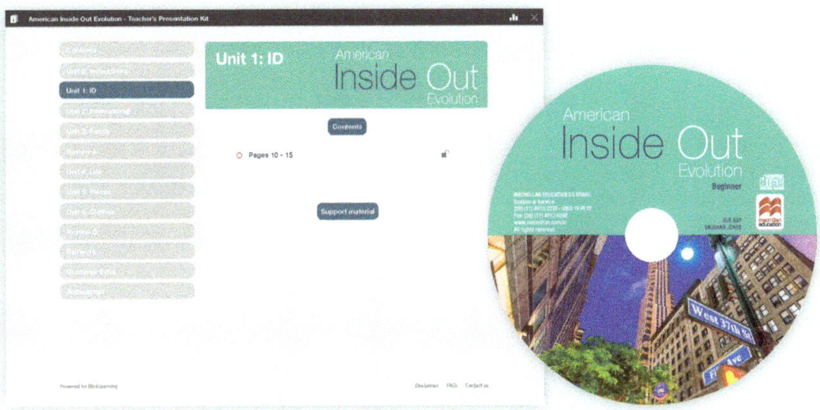

For the Student:
A typical Student's Book unit

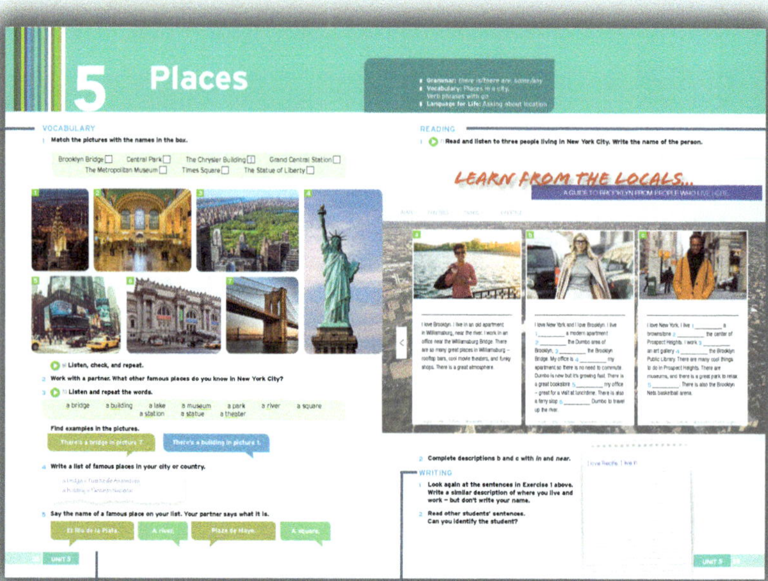

VOCABULARY

- Vocabulary is presented in a meaningful context and is related to the topics in the unit. It is supported by clear pictures to help acquisition.
- There are practice activities to expand the students' knowledge of particular lexical sets to give them opportunities to use the new vocabulary in social exchanges.
- Students also listen and repeat the words before manipulating them in real social contexts.

Opportunities to explore important lexical areas such as collocations and idioms are also integrated into vocabulary sections in upper levels.

READING

A variety of contemporary reading texts have been adapted and graded to appropriately suit each level of the series. They have been selected not only for their language content but also for their interest and appropriacy. The texts are supported by recordings for pedagogical purposes.

SPEAKING

- *American Inside Out Evolution* maintains its essence and provides plenty of opportunities for students to speak throughout the unit using language learned. They are encouraged to exchange meaningful utterances in personalized speaking tasks. The topics provide opportunities for students to engage in conversations bringing their own views, feelings and opinions.
- The Anecdotes are personalized guided speaking tasks which help students develop fluency. Students have the opportunity to talk about their own relevant experiences. They give students a chance to tackle a longer piece of discourse.
- There is one pairwork for every unit which offers further speaking practice. These are dearly labeled for the student and teacher.

WRITING

Motivating writing practice is provided in a task where students follow a model, which is also based on varied texts students need to write on their everyday lives. There is also a comprehensive writing course which runs throughout the Workbook.

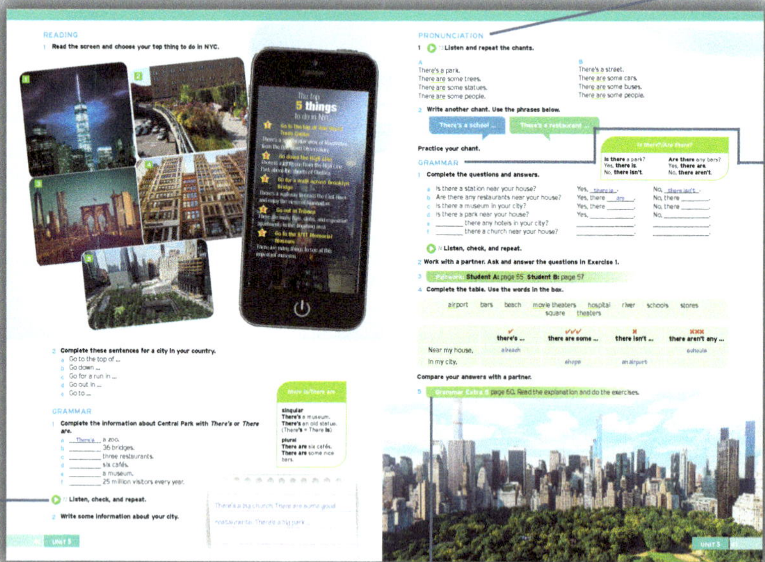

PRONUNCIATION

Pronunciation work on particular areas of sound, stress, and intonation is integrated into every unit.

GRAMMAR

Grammar follows three stages.

- First, students explore new grammatical structures that have been contextualized in the previous section. They focus on the way language works.
- A brief summary of the grammar point is provided in the margin.
- Then, language is explored in realistic and meaningful practices.
- Finally, students use target language for controlled and personalized practice.
- In addition, students are referred to the Grammar Extra pages at the back of the Student's Book for extended explanations and further practice.

LISTENING

The listenings include texts specially written for language learning – dialogues, conversations, monologues. They were carefully designed to develop real life listening skills.

GRAMMAR EXTRA

The Grammar Extra pages at the back of the Student's Book provide a summary of the new grammatical structures, as well as extra practice.

LANGUAGE FOR LIFE

Students are highly interested in the communicative and functional purpose of language. The Language for Life section gives students a portable toolkit of functional language. Here, they notice how language is more than just form. They see language in being used in fun, engaging social situations. The section is recorded on the audio CD to support teaching.

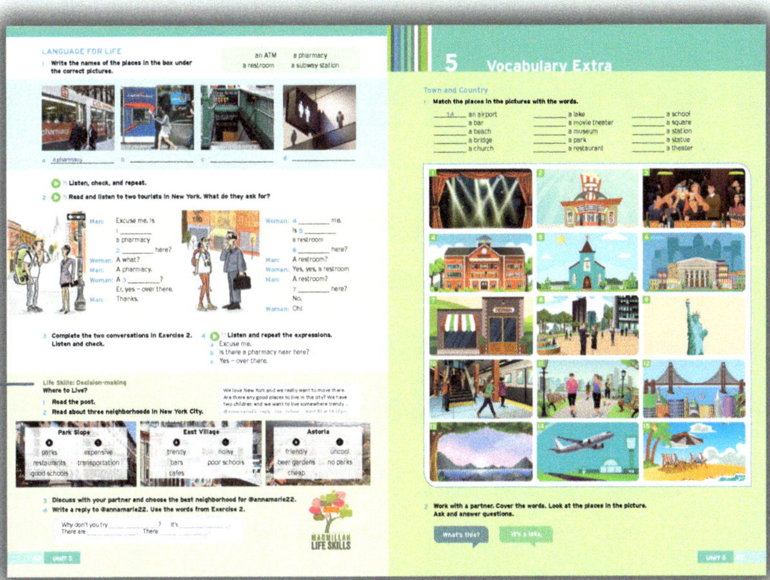

VOCABULARY EXTRA

The Vocabulary Extra pages at the end of every unit recycle the key vocabulary items taught in the unit. This provides students with an activated wordlist and a useful bank of vocabulary.

LIFE SKILLS

- For many adult students, developing life skills alongside language skills is an essential requirement to meet the demands of the contemporary world.
- *American Inside Out Evolution* has a Life Skills section in every unit. Life Skills present activities in order for students to reflect on and discuss about the skills necessary for social and work situations in today's world.

REVIEW

There are Review units in the Student's Book. Each Review unit reviews the new structures and vocabulary taught in the previous teaching units.

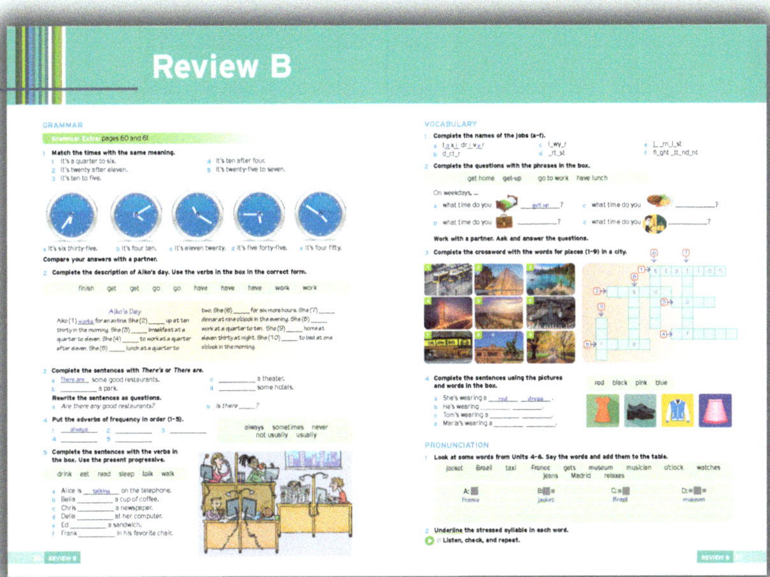

There is one pairwork for every unit which offers further speaking practice.

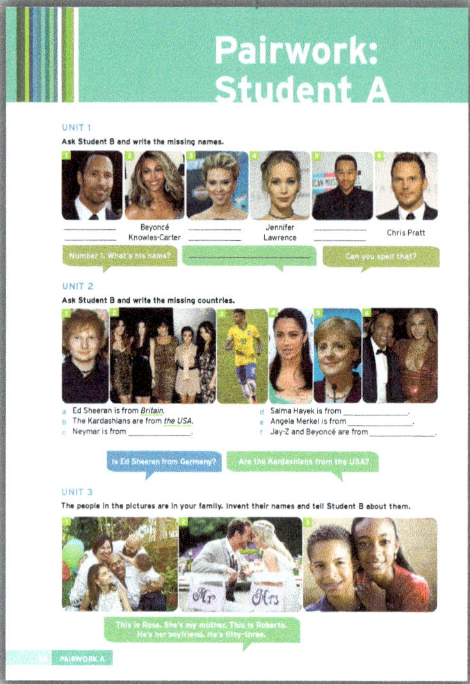

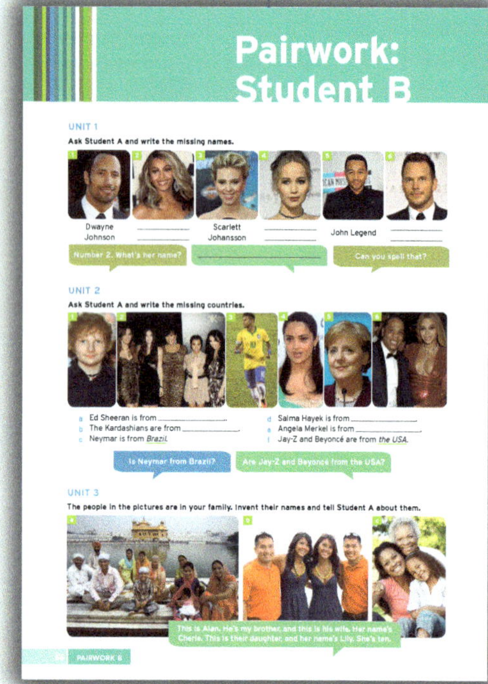

GRAMMAR EXTRA

The Grammar Extra pages at the back of the Student's Book provide a summary of the new grammatical structures, as well as extra practice.

The Workbook provides a review of all the main points in the Student's Book, plus extra listening practice, pronunciation work, and a writing program.

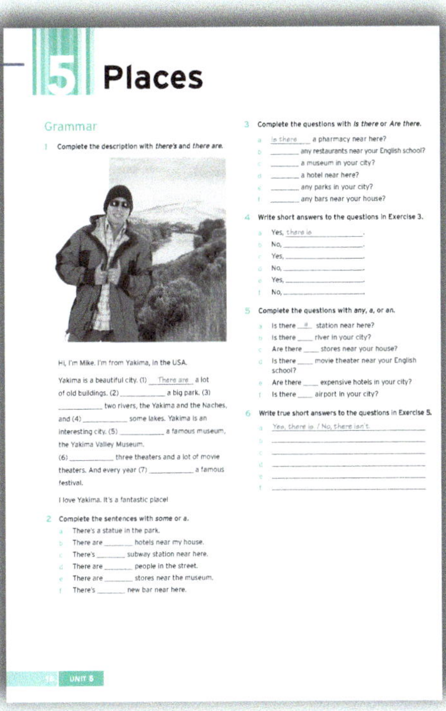

5 Places

Grammar

1 Complete the description with *there's* and *there are*.

Hi, I'm Mike. I'm from Yakima, in the USA.

Yakima is a beautiful city. (1) There are a lot of old buildings. (2) ______ a big park. (3) ______ two rivers, the Yakima and the Naches, and (4) ______ some lakes. Yakima is an interesting city. (5) ______ a famous museum, the Yakima Valley Museum. (6) ______ three theaters and a lot of movie theaters. And every year (7) ______ a famous festival.

I love Yakima. It's a fantastic place!

2 Complete the sentences with *some* or *a*.

a There's a statue in the park.
b There are ______ hotels near my house.
c There's ______ subway station near here.
d There are ______ people in the street.
e There are ______ stores near the museum.
f There's ______ new bar near here.

3 Complete the questions with *Is there* or *Are there*.

a Is there a pharmacy near here?
b ______ any restaurants near your English school?
c ______ a museum in your city?
d ______ a hotel near here?
e ______ any parks in your city?
f ______ any bars near your house?

4 Write short answers to the questions in Exercise 3.

a Yes, there is.
b No, ______.
c Yes, ______.
d No, ______.
e Yes, ______.
f No, ______.

5 Complete the questions with *any*, *a*, or *an*.

a Is there a station near here?
b Is there ____ river in your city?
c Are there ____ stores near your house?
d Is there ____ movie theater near your English school?
e Are there ____ expensive hotels in your city?
f Is there ____ airport in your city?

6 Write true short answers to the questions in Exercise 5.

a Yes, there is. / No, there isn't.
b ______
c ______
d ______
e ______
f ______

18 UNIT 5

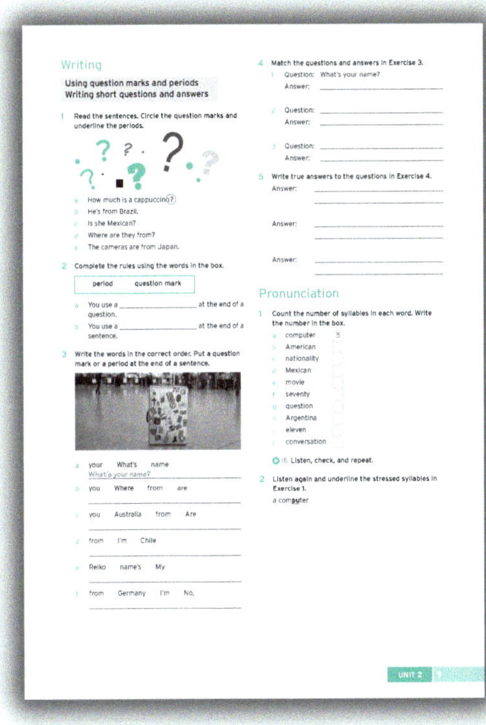

Writing

Using question marks and periods
Writing short questions and answers

1 Read the sentences. Circle the question marks and underline the periods.

a How much is a cappuccino?
b He's from Brazil.
c Is she Mexican?
d Where are they from?
e The cameras are from Japan.

2 Complete the rules using the words in the box.

period question mark

a You use a ______ at the end of a question.
b You use a ______ at the end of a sentence.

3 Write the words in the correct order. Put a question mark or a period at the end of a sentence.

a your What's name
What's your name?
b you Where from are
c you Australia from Are
d from I'm Chile
e Reiko name's My
f from Germany I'm No,

4 Match the questions and answers in Exercise 3.

1 Question: What's your name?
Answer: ______
2 Question: ______
Answer: ______
3 Question: ______
Answer: ______

5 Write true answers to the questions in Exercise 4.

Answer: ______
Answer: ______
Answer: ______

Pronunciation

1 Count the number of syllables in each word. Write the number in the box.

a computer 3
b American
c nationality
d Mexican
e movie
f seventy
g question
h Argentina
i eleven
j conversation

16 Listen, check, and repeat.

2 Listen again and underline the stressed syllables in Exercise 1.

a computer

UNIT 2 9

- The **Digital Student's Book** is a version of the Student's Book in digital. It includes all the student's pages plus the audio tracks for the listening activities. It can be accessed online and offline on computer and tablets.
- The **Digital Workbook** is a version of the Workbook in digital. It includes all the workbook pages plus the audio tracks for the listening activities. It can be accessed online and offline on computer and tablets.
- A free **app** gives students the opportunity for extra classroom practice on the move.
- The **companion website** www.macmillan.com.br/americaninsideoutevolution contains information about the course, its authors and access to resources.

For the Teacher

Teacher's Edition

The Teacher's Edition contains:

An Introduction

Practical methodology

Common European Framework of Reference (CEFR) checklists

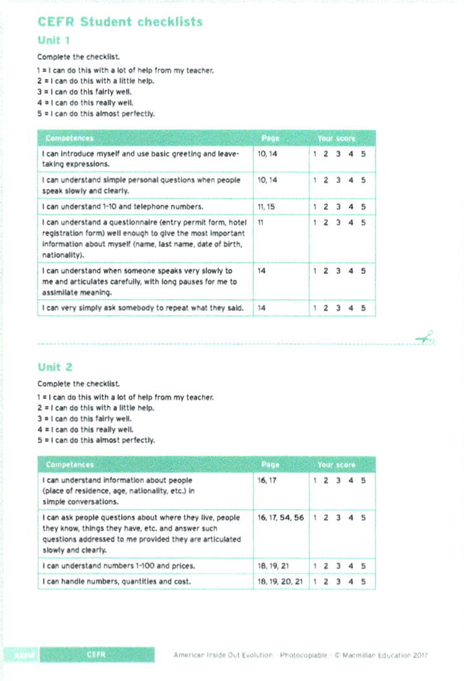

Complete teaching notes with answer keys

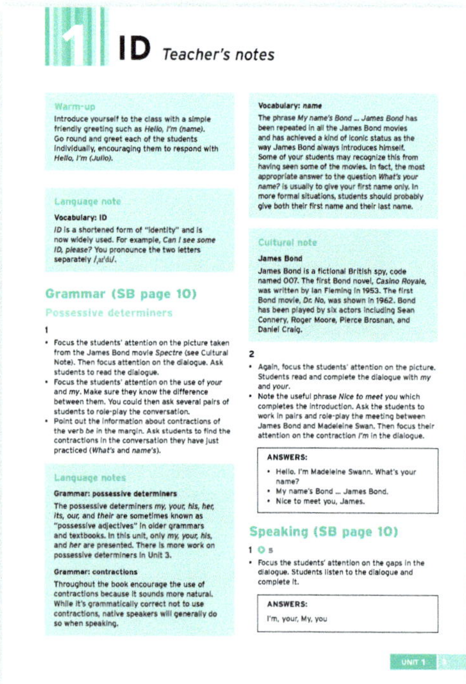

Class CD set

The Class CD contains:

- The dialogues and listening activities from the Student's Book
- Pronunciation activities
- Recordings of the reading texts

- The **Teacher's Presentation Kit** contains Student's Digital Book with audio and answers and with tools that can be used with an Interactive Whiteboard or Data Projector.
- A **Test Generator** is a tool for teachers to edit their own tests.
- The **Extra Resources** are links to tests and a bank of extra photocopiable grammar, vocabulary and communicative activities.
- The **companion website** www.macmillan.com.br/americaninsideoutevolution contains information about the course, its authors and access to resources.

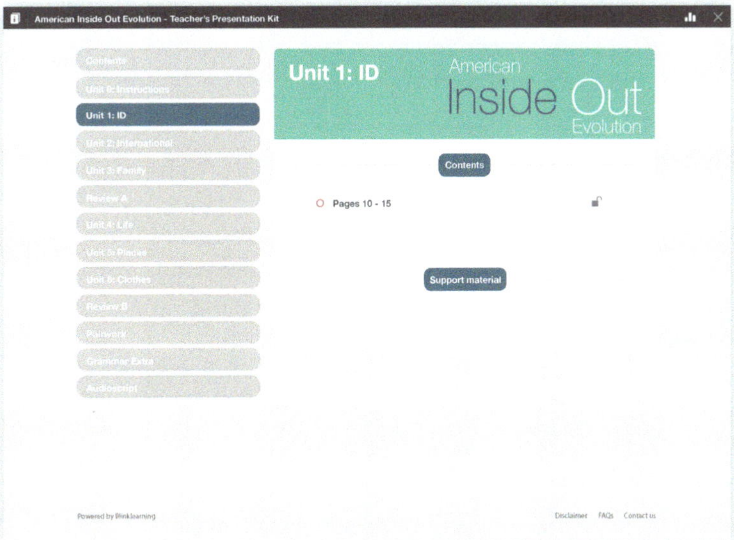

Practical Methodology

Teaching beginners

In this age of the internet, international travel, and world-dominance of English-language rock music, "real" or "absolute" beginners are relatively rare. Most students have at least some prior knowledge of the language, even if it's only a set phrase like *Don't worry, be happy*. In the Beginner level, drawing on our own experience of teaching beginners, and having talked to many English teachers teaching beginners in a wide variety of contexts, we decided that it was best to assume no prior knowledge of the language. We opted for a building-block approach—low and slow—where the content of each unit builds on the previous one, and where the grammar and vocabulary are frequently and systematically reviewed and recycled.

Right from the start

Every teacher has their own way of setting up their classroom, interacting with their students, and conducting their lessons. Here are a few things we've found useful to bear in mind in our beginner classrooms.

The right atmosphere

It's important to do everything you can to create a supportive learning environment. Start by memorizing every student's name and learn as much information as you can about them.

Beginners are often shy about speaking in English. As anyone who has learned a foreign language will know, in the very early stages it takes a great deal of courage to open your mouth and say something. Yet we know that the sooner you start, the more practice you get, the more confident you feel, and the easier it becomes.

In this Beginner level we've used a number of strategies to help build up the students' confidence. Students aren't required to use new language before they've had a chance to listen and repeat words and phrases chorally. "Drilling" is the technique most teachers use to help their students get their tongues around new language. However, when you're focusing on form, it doesn't follow that you have to abandon meaning. In this textbook, language practice, however controlled, is always meaningful.

- Instructions are simple and the same ones are repeated throughout the course.
- Activity types are repeated, especially in the grammar sections, so that the students get used to what is expected of them.
- Students are encouraged to work in pairs and groups, so that they can rehearse the language "in private" rather than be immediately required to speak in the more intimidating arena of the class.

Beginners need much more time to think. It's perfectly normal to have moments of silence while students absorb and process new information, write down new vocabulary from the board, or think about their answers. Don't be afraid of the "pregnant pause"!

The right environment

Your classroom might be the only exposure to English that students get. Make that exposure as rich as you can by decorating the walls with maps and posters. Here are some further ideas.

- Stick up useful formulaic phrases. For example, phrases from Unit 1 Language for Life: *Can you spell that please?*, *Can you repeat that please?*, or Unit 4 expressions: *What's .... ?*, *I don't understand.*, etc.
- Keep a "wordbox" on your table, where words or phrases that come up in the lesson are recorded on strips of paper and put in the box. Alternatively, you could institute the "class scribe" idea. One student in the class is given the role of recording any new language that comes up during the lesson that isn't necessarily the target language of that lesson. This record is then photocopied for everyone in the class, including the teacher who can use the data for review activities. The role of class scribe is rotated.
- Introduce your students to simplified graded readers. Many of them now come with audio. This is invaluable input. Get your students hooked on books!

- Use English in the classroom. It's very tempting to slip into the students' language—particularly if you're teaching beginners in a monolingual situation. Try to use the L1 only for an occasional quick translation or brief explanation.

The right learning skills

If this is their first experience of learning a second language, or if they haven't been very successful in their previous attempts, beginners need some help with learning strategies. Here are some thoughts.

- Spend time encouraging students to experiment with how they record words and phrases from the lesson. Get them to draw the word rather than translate it. They're then associating the word with the concept rather than with another word. Make sure they note the part of speech—verb, noun, adjective, etc. Tell them to find a way of noting the pronunciation of the word, either using phonetic script, or by developing their own system. Ask them to write complete personalized sentences putting the new word or phrase in a real context and thereby making it more memorable.
- A dictionary is a very important language learning tool and most students will buy one. Beginners prefer a bilingual dictionary as this provides them with a quick translation of the word they need. Although at beginner level most of the vocabulary they need is straightforward, it's important to begin teaching them good dictionary skills.

The right amount of practice

In our experience of teaching beginners, the most successful lessons consist of a manageable amount of new input, and then a lot of meaningful practice. For this reason, we've tried to provide maximum practice activities in this textbook, both in the Student's Book and in the other supporting components.

The top 10 activities for beginners

These tried and trusted activities can be used as lead-ins, warmers, fillers, pair-forming activities, or for review and recycling. Most of them require very little or no preparation and can be adapted to cover a wide variety of different language points. You may be familiar with some of the ideas and others may be new. In any event, we hope they provide a useful extension to your teaching repertoire. They certainly get used and re-used in our own classrooms!

It is always useful to have a stock of small white cards and access to a stock of pictures. Magazine pictures are ideal, and can be filed in alphabetical order according to topics.

Alternatively, use the pictures in the Vocabulary Extra section at the end of each unit in the Student's Book.

1 Standing in line

a Alphabetical order

Aim

This is a great way to review *What's your first name/ last name?* after Unit 1.

Preparation

None.

Procedure

- Write three names of students in your class on the board. Underline the first letter of each name, and re-write the names in alphabetical order. Then ask all the students to stand up and put themselves in alphabetical order according to the first letter of their first name.
- Show the class where the line should begin. Encourage them to ask one another *What's your first name?* so that they can put themselves in order. Once they've lined up, check that they're in the correct order by asking them to take it in turns down the line to say *My name's ...*
- Repeat the same procedure using their middle names, their last names, their mother's or father's first name, etc.

b Numerical order

Aim

To recycle numbers.

Preparation

You'll need one card for each student in the class. On each card, write a number that you want to practice.

Procedure

- Ask the students to stand up and take a card each. On the card there is a number. Tell them not to show it to anyone. Ask them to repeat their number aloud until they can organize themselves numerically. Show the class where the line should begin with the lowest number. Then, when they're in line, ask them to hold up their card and say their number to check they're in the correct order.

- Here are some more ideas for line-ups:

1 To practice dates and months: line up in order of the date and month of birth.

2 To practice saying times: hand out a clock face with a different time on it to each student in the class. Ask them to line up in chronological order by saying the time on their clock.

3 To recycle vocabulary: hand out one picture card to each student. Ask them to line up according to the first letter of the word it represents by saying their word aloud.

4 To recycle vocabulary: divide the class into groups, mix up the letters of a word and give one letter to each student in the group. Call out the complete word and ask them to get into the correct order to spell the word.

5 To review word order: mix up the words of a sentence and give one word to each student in the group. Ask them to arrange themselves in the correct order to make a sentence by saying their word aloud.

Follow-up

Once the students have completed a line-up activity, you can divide them into pairs or small groups before they sit down by asking them to work with the student(s) they're standing next to. This works well in a class where students always tend to sit in the same place.

2 Battleships

Aim

To practice the alphabet and review vocabulary.

Preparation

Each student will need a grid of roughly ten to twelve squares across and down (see below). Graph paper is ideal for this activity.

Procedure

Demonstrate the activity by drawing a blank grid on the board. Think of a word or words you want to review and write them onto a different grid on a piece of paper, but don't tell the students what they are yet. You should write the words horizontally, one letter per square, as shown below.

	1	2	3	4	5	6	7	8	9	10	11	12
A	c	o	m	p	u	t	e	r				
B												
C												
D												
E		d	i	c	t	i	o	n	a	r	y	
F												
G												
H												
I			b	a	g							
J												
K												
L												

- Now tell the students that there are some words hidden in the grid. Explain that they need to find the squares with letters in them. Tell them to guess squares by giving letter and number references. For example, C-2, F-12, J-4, etc. When a student guesses a square with a letter in it, write the letter in the square. Continue like this until they've found all the words.
- Now ask the students to work in pairs. First, they should draw two grids. One of them should remain blank, and on the other they need to write words, but without showing them to their partner. Either you can let the students choose their own words, or you can give them a topic. For example, write three countries / nationalities / jobs / classroom objects / names.
- When they've written their words, tell the students to take turns naming a square on their partner's grid. If there's a letter in the square, their partner should say what the letter is and they should write it in the blank grid.
- As soon as they think they know their partner's word, they can guess. If it's wrong, they miss a turn.

3 Hangman

Aim

This game reviews vocabulary and practices the alphabet, so it's a perfect game for beginners.

Preparation

None.

Procedure

- The game can be played as a whole group activity, but also in pairs or small groups when the students know the game. The students can use any vocabulary they know, or you can limit it by telling them to choose from a category. For example, food or a famous person, a verb, or a place.
- Demonstrate on the board. Choose a word for the students to find. For example, *computer*. Write up on the board: _ _ _ _ _ _ _ _.
- Ask the students to guess a letter. If necessary, suggest a letter yourself, for example the letter E and then write it above the appropriate line: _ _ _ _ _ _ E _.
- Ask the students for another letter. If they suggest a letter which is in the word, write it in the appropriate place. If they suggest a letter which isn't in the word, begin to draw the hangman with a vertical line. For the second incorrect guess, draw the horizontal support. For the third, the rope, the fourth is a circle for the head, then a line for the body, one arm, then the second arm, then a leg and finally the second leg.

- If they find the word before the hangman is complete, they win. However, if the hangman is complete, then they lose.

4 Category dictation

Aim

This game reviews vocabulary and practices the alphabet, so it's a perfect game for beginners.

Preparation

Choose the language you want to review and devise a way of categorizing it into two or more categories.

Procedure

- Write the category headings on the board and ask the students to copy them onto a piece of paper. Two simple categories is usually best. More than three can get complicated. Then dictate the words (ten-twelve maximum) slowly and clearly, and ask the students to write them down in the correct category.

  For example, you want to review jobs. Your categories might be jobs you do inside and jobs you do outside. So, write the following on the board and ask the students to copy it down.

Inside	Outside

- Then dictate the words: e.g., *a farmer*, *a teacher*, *a doctor*, *a taxi driver*, etc. The students write down the words in the correct category. When you've dictated ten or twelve words, ask the students to compare their lists. When they've done this, ask them to call out their answers and write them on the board in the correct category, so that they can check the spelling. Alternatively, you could ask the students to take turns writing the answers on the board.
- Here are some more ideas for categories:

1 Review common objects.
Suggested categories: *Singular and Plural*; *In the classroom* and *Not in the classroom*; *In my pocket/bag* and *Not in my pocket/bag*, etc.

2 Review numbers.
Suggested categories: *1 to 20* and *20 to 100*; *Even numbers* and *Odd numbers*

3 Review clothes.
Suggested categories: *Top to bottom* and *Bottom to top*; *Inside* and *Outside*

5 Chain memorization

Aim

This memory activity can be used to review vocabulary or a grammatical structure. It's also very useful for beginners, because it gives them an opportunity to get their tongues around longer utterances.

Preparation

Some simple prompt cards can be helpful, but they aren't essential.

Procedure

- If you have a very large group, it's better to split the group into two or three smaller groups, so that everyone has the opportunity to speak before the sentences get too long!
- First, demonstrate how the game will work before you split the group. For example, to practice *There's / There are* prepare prompt cards based on the vocabulary of the lesson, in this case, features of a city. Model the phrase *In my city, there's a ...* , turn over a card and add the relevant word, for example, *statue*. Ask the first student to repeat *In my city, there's a statue.*
- As they finish, add the words and *there ...* , and turn over another card indicating that you want the next student to add this to the sentence. For example, *In my city there's a statue and there's a museum.* Repeat this procedure with several students. Encourage them to memorize the sentence as it grows. If they falter, you can show them the card as a prompt.
- When they've understood how the activity works, split the class into groups and if necessary, give a set of prompt cards to each group. Alternatively, the students can choose the words to add to the sentence themselves.

6 Mingle drills

Aim

To provide controlled practice of new language in a drill-like way, and to give students the opportunity to repeat the same language with several different partners.

Preparation

Organize your classroom so that the students can move around and speak to one another. Prepare one prompt card for each student in the class. The prompts will depend on the language you want to practice. See Procedure bullet point 2 below for examples of cue cards.

Procedure

- Tell the students that they're going to spend ten to fifteen minutes practicing the new language, and that you're going to show them how to do this.
- Give one card to each student in the class, and keep one for yourself. Write a sample dialogue on the board. Point to the part of the dialogue to be supplied by the picture or word prompts on the card. For example:

side 1	side 2	Sample dialogue on board
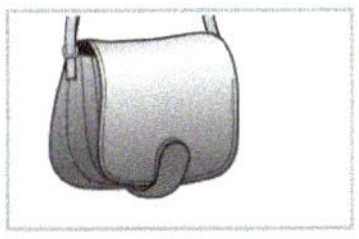	It's a bag.	A: *What's this?* B: *It's a bag.*
side 1	side 2	Sample dialogue on board
	Mike	A: *What does Mike do?* B: *He's a taxi driver.*
side 1	side 2	Sample dialogue on board
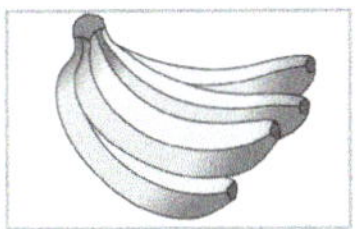	?	A: *Do you like bananas?* B: *Yes, I do.*

- Explain that the language will change according to the prompt on the card. Show the students how to hold their cards. This is important because cards must be held in such a way that when the students are talking to a partner, they're both able to see each other's cards.

- Choose a confident student to demonstrate the activity with you. Then ask two or three pairs of students to demonstrate the dialogue.
- Ask all the students to stand up and to go around the class or group, repeating the dialogue with as many different partners as possible, and using their cards as prompts.
- Stop the activity after a few moments. Ask the students to either exchange cards with another student, or to turn their card around so that the students get the opportunity to make new responses.
- A mingle drill is a controlled practice activity and it's important that the students use the language accurately. Therefore, while the students are doing the drill, go around the class and correct any mistakes in grammar and pronunciation.

7 Crosswords

Aim

This activity is good for reviewing lexical sets and can help with spelling.

Preparation

Choose a lexical set you want to review. For example, *countries* or *nationalities, colors, jobs, clothes*, etc.

Procedure

- Students work in pairs. They'll need a piece of paper, preferably graph paper with squares on it.
- Choose a topic, for example, *nationalities*.
- Student A writes "Across" words, and Student B writes "Down" words.
- It's a good idea to provide the first word across, and make sure that it's a long one. Student B then adds another nationality down the paper from top to bottom. This word must intersect with the nationality word written across the page.
- Student A then writes another nationality across that intersects with the nationality Student B has written down. Students continue taking it in turns to write in their words.

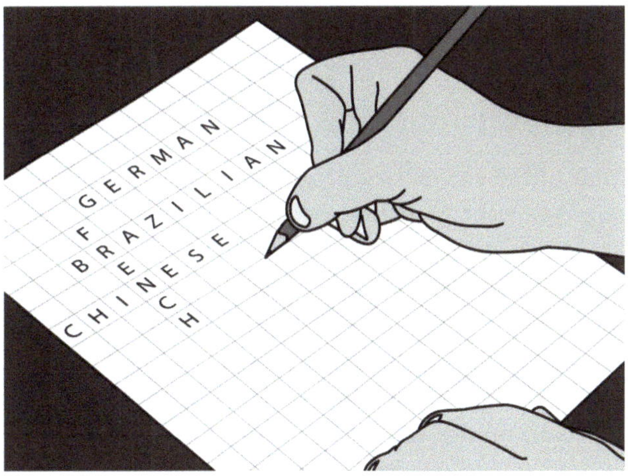

- The students build up a crossword until they can't think of any more nationalities. (You could make it into a game by saying that the last person to write a nationality is the winner.) Note that the students must leave one square empty between each word - this is why it's better and clearer to use squared paper.

8 TPR (Total Physical Response)

Aim

To give students the opportunity to show that they understand language without having to respond orally.

Preparation

Provide cue cards or realia as required.

Procedure

- Minimal pairs for pronunciation practice: for each student, prepare a set of cue cards for pairs of words that students often confuse, for example *hat* and *hot*, *here* and *hair*, *know* and *now*, etc. Hand out a set to each student. Read out a word and ask the students to hold up the word they hear. This also works well with numbers *13/30*, *14/40*, etc.
- *Stand up / Sit down* to show comprehension: in a listening activity, ask different students to listen for different words. Ask them to stand up when they hear their word, and sit down when they hear it again. Useful for pop song activities.
- Follow instructions: to practice prepositions of place, and recycle fruit and vegetable vocabulary, bring a bag of fruit and vegetables to the class. Ask the students to arrange the fruit according to your instructions. For example, put the banana next to the apple, etc.

9 Odd one out

Aim

This activity can be used to review almost any language.

Preparation

Think of the vocabulary, pronunciation, or grammar point you want to review.

Procedure

- Write five words on the board and ask the students which one is the odd one out. The students then explain why, either in the L1 or in the L2. This usually relates to the meaning of the word.

blue	dog	pink	red	yellow

dog is the odd one out because it's an animal. The other words are colors.

- Note that it doesn't matter if the students can't explain in perfect English why *dog* is the odd one out. The important thing is that they're looking at and thinking about the words you want to review.
- You can use this format to practice and review all sorts of things. Here are some examples.

1 For meaning:
sister / grandfather / daughter / wife / mother
grandfather is the odd one out because he's a man. The other words describe women.

2 For spelling:
pen / book / bag / telephone / diary
diary is the odd one out because you spell the plural *ies*. The other words you just add *s*.

3 For pronunciation: sounds
A / I / H / J / K
I is the odd one out because the vowel sound is different.

4 For pronunciation: stress
hospital / banana / potato / computer
hospital is the odd one out because the stress is on the first syllable. The other words have the stress on the second syllable.

5 For grammar:
work / go / see / take / swim
work is the odd one out because it's regular. The other verbs are irregular.

10 Board bingo

Aim

This activity is good for reviewing any type of vocabulary.

Preparation

Write down twelve to fifteen words you want to review on the board.

Procedure

- Ask the students to choose five of the words and write them down. When they've done that, tell the students that you're going to read out words in random order and that they should cross out one of their words if they hear it. When they've crossed out all five words, they shout *Bingo!* Make sure you keep a record of the words you call out so that you can check the students' answers.
- You can make this more challenging by reading out dictionary definitions of the words rather than the words themselves. (Or if you teach a monolingual class then you could read out a translation of each word).
- At the beginning of the course, you could simplify the activity by writing up single letters (especially the vowels) or numbers (or a mixture of cardinal and ordinal numbers).

Key concepts

The following excerpts are from *An A-Z of ELT* by Scott Thornbury (Macmillan Books for Teachers, 2006). They give clear authoritive definitions and explanations of some of the most important concepts in this textbook.

Contents

- classroom interaction
- collocation
- communicative activity
- context
- drill
- dynamics: group, classroom
- fluency
- focus on form
- function
- grammar teaching
- learner-centered instruction, learner-centeredness
- learning style
- listening
- motivation
- noticing
- personalization
- practice
- pronunciation teaching
- reading
- speaking
- task
- vocabulary teaching
- writing

classroom interaction *methodology*

Classroom interaction is the general term for what goes on between the people in the classroom, particularly when it involves language. In traditional classrooms, most interaction is initiated by the teacher, and learners either respond individually, or in unison. Teacher-centered interaction of this kind is associated with *transmissive* teaching, such as a lecture or presentation, where the teacher *transmits* the content of the lesson to the learners.

In order to increase the amount of student involvement and interaction, teacher–learner interaction is often combined with **pairwork** and **groupwork**, where learners interact among themselves in pairs or small groups. Other kinds of interaction include *mingling* or *milling*. Pairwork and groupwork are associated with a more **learner-centered** approach. Rather than passively receiving the lesson content, the learners are actively engaged in using language and discovering things for themselves. The value of pairwork and groupwork has been reinforced by the belief that **interaction** facilitates language learning. Some would go as far as to say that it is *all* that is required.

The potential for classroom interaction is obviously constrained by such factors as the number of students, the size of the room, the furniture, and the purpose or type of activity. Not all activities lend themselves to pairwork or groupwork. Some activities, such as reading, are best done as *individual work*. On the other hand, listening activities (such as listening to an audio recording, or to the teacher) favour a *whole class* format, as do grammar presentations. The whole class is also an appropriate form of organization when reviewing the results of an activity, as, for example, when spokespersons from each group are reporting on the results of a discussion or survey.

The success of any classroom interaction will also depend on the extent to which the learners know what they are meant to be doing and why, which in turn depends on how clearly and efficiently the interaction has been set up. Pair- and groupwork can be a complete waste of time if learners are neither properly prepared for it, nor sure of its purpose or outcome.

Finally, the success of pair- and groupwork will depend on the kind of group **dynamics** that have been established. Do the students know one another? Are they happy working together? Do they mind working without constant teacher supervision? Establishing a productive classroom dynamic may involve making decisions as to who works with whom. It may also mean deliberately staging the introduction of different kinds of interactions, starting off with the more controlled, teacher-led interactions before, over time, allowing learners to work in pairs and finally in groups.

collocation *vocabulary*

If two words *collocate*, they frequently occur together. The relation between the words may be grammatical, as when certain verbs collocate with particular prepositions, such as *depend on*, *account for*, *abstain from*, or when a verb, like *make*, *take*, or *do*, collocates with a noun, as in *make an arrangement*, *take advantage*, *do the shopping*. The collocation may also be lexical, as when two **content words** regularly co-occur, as in *a broad hint*, *a narrow escape* (but not **a wide hint* or **a tight escape*). The strength of the collocation can vary: *a broad street* or *a narrow path* are weak collocations, since both elements can co-occur with lots of other words: *a broad river*, *a busy street*, etc. *Broad hint* and *narrow escape* are stronger. Stronger still are combinations where one element rarely occurs without the other, as in *moot point*, *slim pickings* and *scot free*. Strongest of all are those where both elements never or rarely occur without the other, such as *dire straits* and *spick and span*. These have acquired the frozen status of *fixed expressions*.

Unsurprisingly, learners lack intuitions as to which words go with which, and this accounts for many errors, such as *You can completely enjoy it* (instead of *thoroughly*), *On Saturday we made shopping* (instead of *went*), and *We went the incorrect way* (for *wrong*). Using texts to highlight particular collocations, and teaching new words in association with their most frequent collocations are two ways of approaching the problem. Nowadays learners' dictionaries also include useful collocational information.

communicative activity *methodology*

A communicative activity is one in which real communication occurs. Communicative activities belong to that generation of classroom **activities** that emerged in response to the need for a more **communicative approach** in the teaching of second languages. (In their more evolved form as **tasks**, communicative activities are central to **task-based learning**). They attempt to import into a practice activity the key features of "real-life" communication. These are:

- *purposefulness:* speakers are motivated by a communicative goal (such as getting information, making a request, giving instructions) and not simply by the need to display the correct use of language for its own sake
- *reciprocity:* to achieve a purpose, speakers need to interact, and there is as much need to listen as to speak
- *negotiation:* following from the above, they may need to check and **repair** the communication in order to be understood by each other
- *unpredictability:* neither the process, nor the outcome, nor the language used in the exchange, is entirely predictable
- *heterogeneity:* participants can use any communicative means at their disposal; in other words, they are not restricted to the use of a pre-specified grammar item.

And, in the case of spoken language in particular:

- *synchronicity:* the exchange takes place in real time

The best known communicative activity is the *information gap* activity. Here, the information necessary to complete the task is either in the possession of just one of the participants, or distributed among them.

In order to achieve the goal of the task, therefore, the learners have to share the information that they have. For example, in a *describe-and-draw* activity, one student has a picture which is hidden from his or her partner. The task is for that student to describe the picture so that the partner can accurately draw it. In a *find-the-difference* task, both students of a pair have pictures (or texts) that are the same apart from some minor details. The goal is to identify these differences. In a *jigsaw activity*, each member of a group has different information. One might have a bus timetable, another a map, and another a list of hotels. They have to share this information in order to plan a weekend break together.

Information gap activities have been criticized on the grounds that they lack **authenticity**. Nor are information gap activities always as productive as might be wished: unsupervised, learners may resort to **communication strategies** in order to simplify the task. A more exploitable information gap, arguably, is the one that exists between the learners themselves, i.e., what they don't know—but might like to know—about one another (➜ **personalization**).

context *linguistics*

The context of a language item is its adjacent language items. In the absence of context, it is often impossible to assign exact meaning to an item. A sentence like *Ben takes the bus to work*, for example, could have past, present, or future reference, depending on the context:

> I know this guy called Ben. One day Ben *takes the bus to work*, and just as ...
> Most days Ben *takes the bus to work*, but sometimes he rides his bike ...
> If *Ben takes the bus to work* tomorrow, he'll be late, because there's a strike ...

Likewise, a sentence like *You use it like this* is meaningless in the absence of a context. By the same token, a word or sentence in one context can have a very different meaning in another. The sign *NO BICYCLES* in a public park means something different to *NO BICYCLES* outside a bicycle rental shop. It is sometimes necessary to distinguish between different kinds of context. On the one hand, there is the context of the accompanying **text**, sometimes called the *co-text*. The cotext of this sentence, for example, includes the sentences that precede and follow it, as well as the paragraph of which it forms a part. It is the co-text that offers clues as to the meaning of unfamiliar vocabulary in a text.

The *situational context* (also *context of situation, context of use*), on the other hand, is the physical and temporal setting in which an instance of language use occurs. The typical context for the spoken question *Are you being served?* is in a shop, for example. Both co-text and context influence the production and interpretation of language. **Discourse analysis** studies the relationship between language and co-text, including the way that sentences or utterances are connected. **Pragmatics** studies the relationship between language and its contexts of use, including the way meaning can be inferred by reference to context factors. Various theories have been proposed in order to account for the ways that language choices are determined by contextual factors. One of the best known of these is Michael Halliday's **systemic functional linguistics.** Halliday distinguishes three variables in any context that systematically impact on language choices and which, together, determine a text's **register**:

- the *field*: what the language is being used to talk about, and for what purposes
- the *tenor*: the participants in the language event, and their relationship
- the *mode*: how language is being used in the exchange, e.g. is it written or spoken?

For example, this short text shows the influence of all three factors:

> Do u fancy film either 2nite or 2moro?
> Call me.

The field is "making arrangements about leisure activities", hence the use of words like *film, 2nite (tonight), 2moro (tomorrow).* The tenor is one of familiarity and equality (accounting for the informal *fancy* and the imperative: *call me*); and the mode is that of a written text message, which explains its brevity, its use of abbreviated forms (*u, 2nite*) and the absence of salutations. A change in any of these contextual factors is likely to have a significant effect on the text.

Language learners, it is argued, need to know how these contextual factors correlate with language choices in order to produce language that is appropriate to the context. One way of doing this is to ask them to make changes to a text (such as the text message above) that take into account adjustments to the field, tenor, or mode.

drill *methodology*

A drill is repetitive oral practice of a language item, whether a sound, a word, a phrase or a sentence structure. Drills that are targeted at sentence structures are sometimes called *pattern practice drills*. Drills follow a prompt–response sequence, where the prompt usually comes from the teacher, and the students respond, either in chorus (*a choral drill*) or individually. An *imitation drill* simply involves repeating the prompt, as in:

> **Teacher:** They have been watching TV.
> **Student:** They have been watching TV.

A *substitution drill* requires the students to substitute one element of the pattern with the prompt, making any necessary adjustments:

> **Teacher:** They have been watching TV.
> **Student:** They have been watching TV.
> **Teacher:** She
> **Student:** She has been watching TV.
> **Teacher:** I
> **Student:** I have been watching TV.

etc.

A *variable substitution drill* is the same, but the prompts are not restricted to one element of the pattern:

> **Teacher:** They have been watching TV.
> **Student:** They have been watching TV.
> **Teacher:** She
> **Student:** She has been watching TV.
> **Teacher:** radio
> **Student:** She has been listening to the radio.
> **Teacher:** We
> **Student:** We have been listening to the radio.

etc.

Drills were a defining feature of the **audiolingual** method, and were designed to reinforce good language "habits." The invention of language laboratories allowed sustained drilling without the need for a teacher to supply the prompts. With the demise of audiolingualism, drilling fell from favor. However, many teachers—even those who subscribe to a **communicative approach**—feel the need for some form of repetition practice of the kind that drills provide. This may be for the purpose of developing **accuracy**, or as a form of **fluency** training, ie, in order to develop **automaticity**.

Hence, communicative drills were developed. A communicative drill is still essentially repetitive, and focuses on a particular structure or pattern but it has an *information gap* element built in. Learners can perform the drill in pairs, or as a *milling activity* (**classroom interaction**) and they are required to attend to what they hear as much as what they say. The milling activity popularly known as *Find someone who ...* is one such activity. Students are set the task of finding other students in the class who, for example, can ride a horse, can speak French, can play the guitar, etc. They mill around, asking questions of the type *Can you ...?* until they have asked all the other students their questions, and then they report their findings.

dynamics: group, classroom *methodology*

Dynamics are the actions and interactions, both conscious and unconscious, that take place between members of a group, whether the whole class or subgroups. Group dynamics are instrumental in forging a productive and motivating classroom environment. They are determined by such factors as: the composition of the group (including the age, sex, and relative status of the members, as well as their different attitudes, beliefs, learning styles and abilities); the patterns of relationships between members of the group, including how well they know each other, and the roles they each assume, such as group leader, spokesperson, etc; physical factors such as the size of the group and the way it is seated; and the tasks that the group are set, e.g.: Does the task require everyone to contribute? Does it encourage co-operation or competition? Are the goals of the task clear to the group members?

Ways that the teacher can promote a positive group (and class) dynamic include:

- ensuring all class or group members can see and hear one another, and that they know (and use) each other's names
- keeping groups from getting too big—three to six members is optimal
- setting—or negotiating—clear rules for groupwork, such as using only the target language, giving everyone a turn to speak, allowing individuals to "pass" if they don't want to say anything too personal
- using "ice-breaking" activities to encourage interaction, laughter, and relaxation
- ensuring that group tasks are purposeful, interactive, and collaborative
- personalizing tasks, i.e., setting tasks that involve the sharing of personal experiences and opinions
- defining the roles and responsibilities within the group, and varying these regularly, e.g. by appointing a different spokesperson each time
- monitoring groupwork in progress, and being alert to any possible conflicts or tensions between members, and reconstituting groups, if necessary
- discussing the importance of groupwork with learners, and getting feedback on group processes

fluency *SLA*

If someone is said to be fluent in a language, or to speak a language fluently, it is generally understood that they are able to speak the language idiomatically and accurately, without undue pausing, without an intrusive accent, and in a manner appropriate to the context. In fact, research into listeners' perceptions of fluency suggests that fluency is primarily the ability to produce and maintain speech in *real time*.

To do this, fluent speakers are capable of:

- appropriate pausing, i.e.:
  - their pauses may be long but are not frequent
  - their pauses are usually filled, e.g. with **pause fillers** like *erm*, *you know*, *sort of*
  - their pauses occur at meaningful transition points, e.g. at the intersections of clauses or phrases, rather than midway in a phrase
- long runs, i.e., there are many syllables and words between pauses

All of the above factors depend on the speaker having a well-developed grammar, an extensive vocabulary, and, crucially, a store of memorized *chunks*. Being able to draw on this store of chunks means not having to depend on grammar to construct each utterance from scratch. This allows the speaker to devote **attention** to other aspects of the interaction, such as planning ahead. Speakers also use a number of "tricks" or *production strategies* to convey the illusion of fluency. One such strategy is disguising pauses by filling them, or by repeating a word or phrase.

Some proponents of the **communicative approach** re-defined fluency so as to distinguish it from **accuracy**. Fluency came to mean "communicative effectiveness", regardless of formal accuracy or speed of delivery. Activities that are communicative, such as information-gap activities, are said to be *fluency-focused*. This is the case even for activities that produce short, halting utterances. Separating accuracy and fluency, and defining the latter as *communicative* language use, is misleading, though. There are many speech events whose communicativeness depends on their accuracy. Air traffic control talk is just one. Moreover, many learners aspire to being more than merely communicative.

Classroom activities that target fluency need to prepare the learner for real-time speech production. Learning and memorizing lexical chunks, including useful conversational gambits, is one approach. **Drills** may help here, as will some types of **communicative activity** that involve repetition. Research has also shown that fluency improves the more times a **task** is repeated. Fluency may also benefit from activities that manage to distract learners' attention away from formal accuracy so that they are not tempted to slow down. (This has been called "parking their attention"). Some interactive and competitive language **games** have this effect. **Drama** activities, such as roleplays, recreate conditions of real-time language use, and are therefore good for developing fluency. Finally, learners can achieve greater fluency from learning a repertoire of **communication strategies**, i.e., techniques for getting around potential problems caused by a lack of the relevant words or structures.

focus on form *SLA*

When learners focus on form, they direct conscious attention to some formal feature of the language **input**. The feature may be the fact that the past of *has* is *had*, or that *enjoy* is followed by verb forms ending in *-ing*, or that adjectives do not have plural forms in English. The learners' attention may be self-directed, or it may be directed by the teacher or by another learner. Either way, it has been argued that a focus on **form** is a necessary condition for language learning. Simply focusing on the **meaning** of the input is not enough. Focusing on form is, of course, not a new idea: most teaching methods devote a great deal of time to the forms of the language, e.g. when new grammar items are presented. But the term *focus on form* captures the fact that this focus can, theoretically, occur at any stage in classroom instruction. Thus, **correction**, especially in the form of negative **feedback**, is a kind of focus on form. In fact, some researchers argue that the most effective form focus is that which arises incidentally, in the context of communication, as when the teacher quickly elicits a correction during a classroom discussion. This incidental approach contrasts with the more traditional and deliberate approach, where teaching is based on a **syllabus** of graded structures (or *forms*), and these are pre-taught in advance of activities designed to practice them. This traditional approach is called– by some researchers–a *focus on forms*.

function *linguistics*

The function of a language item is its communicative purpose. Language is more than simply **forms** and their associated meanings (i.e., **usage**). It is also the communicative **uses** to which these forms and meanings are put. These two sentences, for example, share the same forms, but function quite differently:

[in an email]	*Thank you for sending me the disk.*
[a notice in a taxi]	*Thank you for not smoking.*

The function of the first is *expressing thanks*, while the second is more like a *prohibition*. Likewise, the same function can be expressed by different forms:

[a notice in a taxi]	*Thank you for not smoking.*
[a sign in a classroom]	*No smoking.*

Thus, there is no one-to-one match between form and function. Assigning a function to a text or an utterance usually requires knowledge of the **context** in which the text is used. The study of how context and function are interrelated is called **pragmatics**.

Communicative functions can be categorized very broadly and also at increasing levels of detail. The "big" functions, or macrofunctions, describe the way language is used in very general terms. These include the use of language for *expressive* purposes (e.g. poetry), for *regulatory* purposes (e.g. for getting people to do things), for *interpersonal* purposes (e.g. for socializing), and for *representational* purposes (e.g. to inform). More useful, from the point of view of designing language syllabuses, are microfunctions. These are usually expressed as **speech acts**, such as *agreeing* and *disagreeing, reporting, warning, apologizing, thanking, greeting*, etc. Such categories form the basis of **functional syllabuses**, a development associated with the **communicative approach**. They often appear as one strand of a coursebook **syllabus**. Functions differ from notions in that the latter describe areas of meaning—such as *ability, duration, quantity, frequency,* etc.—rather than the uses to which these meanings are put.

One way to teach functions is to adopt a "phrasebook" approach, and teach useful ways of expressing common functions (what are called *functional exponents*), such as *Would you like ...? (inviting)* and *Could you ..., please? (requesting)*. More memorable, though, is to teach these expressions in the contexts of **dialogues**, so that the functional exponents are associated not only with common situations in which they are used, but with related functions (such as *accepting* and *refusing*). The term *function*, in contrast to **form**, is also used in linguistics, specifically with regard to the functions of the different elements of a **clause** (such as subject and object).

grammar teaching *methodology*

Like the word **grammar** itself, the topic of grammar teaching is a controversial one, and teachers often take opposing views. Historically, language teaching methods have positioned themselves along a scale from "zero grammar" to "total grammar", according to their approach to grammar teaching. Proponents of *natural methods*, who model their approach to teaching second languages on the way that first languages are acquired, reject any explicit teaching of grammar at all. (They may, however, teach according to a grammar **syllabus**, even if no mention of grammar as such is made in the classroom). This implicit approach is common both to the **direct method** and to **audiolingualism**. Through exposure to demonstrations, situations or examples, learners are expected to pick up the rules of grammar by **inductive learning**. At the other end of the spectrum, there are approaches, such as **grammar-translation**, that adopt an explicit and **deductive learning** approach. From the outset, learners are presented with rules which they study and then practise. Occupying a midway point between zero grammar and total grammar is the approach called **consciousness-raising**. Instead of being given rules, learners are presented with language data which challenge them to re-think (and *restructure*) their existing mental grammar. This data might take the form of **input** that has been manipulated in some way. For example, pairs of sentences, such as the following, have to be matched to pictures, forcing learners to discriminate between them, and, in theory, **notice** the difference (**➜ noticing**):

> The Queen drove to the airport.
> The Queen was driven to the airport.

(This is sometimes called a *grammar interpretation task*, or *structured input*.) In order to do the task, learners have to process not just the individual words, but also their grammatical form. That is why this approach to teaching grammar is sometimes called *processing instruction*. There are other researchers who argue that it is by means of manipulating the learner's output, e.g. through productive practice, that mental restructuring is best effected.

The **communicative approach** accommodates different approaches to grammar teaching. Proponents of **task-based** learning, for example, argue that, if the learner is engaged in solving problems using language, then the mental grammar will develop of its own accord. However, advocates of the weaker version of the communicative approach (and the version that is most widespread) justify a role for the pre-teaching of grammar in advance of production. This view finds support in **cognitive learning theory**, which suggests that conscious attention to grammatical form (called **focus on form**) speeds up language learning, and is a necessary corrective against premature **fossilization.** There is some debate, though, as to whether this form focus should be planned or incidental. Incidental grammar teaching occurs when the teacher deals with grammar issues as and when they come up, e.g. in the form of **correction**, or task **feedback.**

In this way (it is argued) grammar teaching follows the learner's own "syllabus". Such an approach attempts to address one of the dilemmas of grammar teaching: the fact that the learner's mental grammar, and the way it develops, bears only an accidental relation to a formal grammar syllabus.

Nevertheless, the research into these different choices is still inconclusive. It may be the case that some items of grammar respond better to explicit teaching, while others are more easily picked up through exposure. There are also different learner types: some prefer learning and applying rules, while others are happier with a more "deep-end" approach (**➜ learning style**). Most current teaching materials hedge their bets on these issues. They offer both deductive and inductive grammar presentations, and opportunities for incidental as well as for planned learning.

learner-centered instruction, learner-centeredness *methodology*

Learner-centered instruction aims to give learners more say in areas that are traditionally considered the domain of the teacher or of the institution. Learner-centered instruction is true to the spirit of progressive education, including the movement towards providing learners with greater **autonomy.** For example, a learner-centered **curriculum** would involve learners in negotiating decisions relating to the choice of syllabus content, of materials, of activity-types, and of assessment procedures. Learner-centeredness also describes ways of organizing **classroom interaction** so that the focus is directed away from the teacher, and on to the learners, who perform tasks in pairs or small groups. This contrasts with traditional, teacher-centered, classroom interaction. Some writers believe that the dichotomy between learner-centered (= good) and teacher-centered (= bad) is a false one. It might be more useful to talk about *learning-centered instruction*, i.e., instruction which prioritizes sound learning principles. In a learning-centered approach there would be room for both learner-centered *and* teacher-centered interactions.

learning style *psychology*

Your learning style is your preferred way of learning. This style may be influenced by biographical factors (such as how you were taught as a child) or by innately endowed factors (such as whether you have a "good ear" for different sounds). Types of learning style are often presented in the form of polarities (some of which may overlap), such as:

- analytic versus global (or holistic) thinkers, i.e., learners who tend to focus on the details, versus learners who tend to see "the big picture"
- rule-users versus data-gatherers, i.e., learners who learn and apply rules, versus those who prefer exposure to lots of examples
- reflective versus impulsive learners
- group-oriented versus solitary learners
- extrovert versus introverted learners
- verbal versus visual learners
- passive versus active learners

Attempts have been made to group these polarities and relate them to brain lateralization. So, a bias towards left-brain processing correlates with analytic, rule-forming and verbal learners, while a bias towards right-brain processing correlates with their opposite. A less binary view of learning style is that proposed by the psychologist Howard Gardner. He identified at least seven distinct intelligences that all individuals possess but to different degrees. These include the *logical/mathematical*, the *verbal/linguistic*, and the *visual/spatial*. Similarly, proponents of **neuro-linguistic programming** distinguish between different sensory orientations, including the *visual*, *aural* and *kinesthetic* (i.e., related to movement, touch). So far, though, there is no convincing evidence that any of these dispositions correlates with specific learning behaviors. Nor has it been shown that a preference in one area predicts success in language learning. In fact, it is very difficult to separate learning style from other potentially influential factors, such as personality, intelligence, and previous learning experience. Nor is it clear to what extent learning style can be manipulated, e.g. through **learner training**. The best that can be said is that, if the learner's preferred learning style is out of synch with the type of instruction on offer, then success is much less likely than if the two are well matched. This supports the case for an **eclectic** approach, on the one hand, and the individualization of learning, on the other.

listening *methodology*

Listening is the skill of understanding spoken language. It is also the name given to classroom activities that are designed to develop this skill—what are also called *listening comprehension* activities—as in "today we're going to do a listening". Listening is one of the four language **skills**, and, along with **reading**, was once thought of as being a "passive" skill. In fact, although receptive, listening is anything but passive. It is a goal-oriented activity, involving not only processing of the incoming speech signals (called *bottom-up processing*) but also the use of prior knowledge, contextual clues, and expectations (*top-down processing*) in order to create meaning. Among the sub-skills of listening are:

- perceiving and discriminating individual sounds
- segmenting the stream of speech into recognizable units such as words and phrases
- using **stress** and **intonation** cues to distinguish given information from new information
- attending to **discourse markers** and using these to predict changes in the direction of the talk
- guessing the meaning of unfamiliar words
- using clues in the text (such as vocabulary) and context clues to predict what is coming
- making inferences about what is not stated
- selecting key information relevant to the purpose for listening
- integrating incoming information into the mental "picture" (or **schema**) of the speech event so far

Also, since listening is normally interactive, listeners need to be capable of:

- recognizing when speakers have finished their turns, or when it is appropriate to interrupt
- providing ongoing signals of understanding, interest, etc. (*backchanneling*)
- asking for clarification, asking someone to repeat what they have just said, and repairing misunderstandings

These sub-skills exist across languages, so, in theory, learners should be able to transfer them from their first language into their second. In fact, there are a number of reasons why this does not always happen. One is that speakers of different languages process speech signals differently, depending on the phonetic characteristics of the language they are used to. This means that speakers of some languages will find it harder than others to match the spoken word to the way that the word is represented in their mind. They simply do not recognize the word. Another problem is lack of sufficient L2 knowledge, such as vocabulary or grammar. A third problem is that learners may lack the means (and the confidence) to negotiate breakdowns in understanding. Finally, many learners simply lack exposure to spoken language, and therefore have not had sufficient opportunities to experience listening. These problems can be compounded in classrooms because:

- Listening to audio recordings deprives the learners of useful visual information, and allows the learners no opportunity to interact and repair misunderstandings.
- Classroom acoustics are seldom ideal.
- If learners do not know what they are listening for (in the absence, for example, of some pre-set listening task) they may try to process as much information as possible, rather than being selective in their listening. This can lead to listening overload, which in turn can cause inhibiting anxiety.
- Listening texts that have been specially written for classroom use are often simplified. But if this simplification means eliminating a lot of redundant language, such as speaker repetitions, pause fillers and vague language, the density of information that results may make it harder—not easier—to process.

For this reason, the use of audio recordings to develop listening skills needs to be balanced against the advantages of using other media, such as video, and face-to-face interaction with the teacher or another speaker.

Nevertheless, the use of audio recordings is an established part of classroom practice, so it is important to know how to use them to best advantage. The following approach is one that is often recommended:

- Provide some minimum contextual information, e.g. who is talking to whom about what, and why. This helps to compensate for lack of visual information, and allows learners to activate the relevant mental **schema**, which in turn helps top-down processing, including the sub-skill of prediction.
- Pre-teach key vocabulary: this helps with bottom-up processing, although too much help may mean that learners don't get sufficient practice in guessing from context.

- Set some "while-listening" questions. Initially, these should focus on the overall gist of the text. For example: true/false questions, selecting, ordering or matching pictures, ticking items on a list, following a map.
- Play a small section of the recording first, to give learners an opportunity to familiarize themselves with the different voices, and to trigger accurate expectations as to what they will hear.
- Play the recording right through, and then allow learners to consult on the answers to the pre-set task. Check these answers. If necessary, re-play the recording until satisfied that learners have "got the gist".
- Set a more demanding task, requiring more intensive listening, such as listening for detail, or inferring speakers' attitudes, intentions, etc. If the recording is a long one, it may pay to stage the intensive listening in sections. Again, allow learners to consult in pairs, before checking the task in open class.
- On the basis of the learners' success with these tasks, identify problem sections of the recording and return to these, playing and re-playing them, and perhaps eliciting a word-by-word transcription and writing this on the board.
- Distribute copies of the transcript of the recording (if available) and re-play the recording while learners read the transcript. This allows the learners to clear up any remaining problems, and also to match what they hear to what they see.

The above approach can be adapted to suit different kinds of recorded texts and different classroom needs. For higher level learners, for example, it may be counterproductive to make listening too easy. The approach can also be adapted to the use of video, and even to *live listenings*, such as listening to the teacher or a guest.

motivation *psychology*

Motivation is what drives learners to achieve a goal, and is a key factor determining success or failure in language learning. The learner's goal may be a short-term one, such as successfully performing a classroom task, or a long-term one, such as achieving native-like proficiency in the language. With regard to long-term goals, a distinction is often made between *instrumental motivation* and *integrative motivation*. Instrumental motivation is when the learner has a functional objective, such as passing an exam or getting a job. Integrative motivation, on the other hand, is when the learner wants to be identified with the target language community. Intersecting with these two motivational *orientations* are two different *sources* of motivation: *intrinsic* (e.g. the pleasure of doing a task for its own sake) and *extrinsic* (e.g. the "carrot and stick" approach). Another motivational source that has been identified is success: experience of succeeding can result in increased motivation (called *resultative motivation*), which raises the question as to whether motivation is as much a result as a cause of learning.

Various theories of motivation have been proposed. Most of these identify a variety of factors that, in combination, contribute to overall motivation, such as:

- *attitudes*, e.g. to the target language and to speakers of the language
- *goals*, both long-term and short-term, and the learners' *orientation* to these goals
- how much *value* the learner attaches to achieving the goals, especially as weighed against *expectancy of success*; expectancy of success may come from the learners' assessment of their own abilities, and how they account for previous successes or failures
- *self-esteem*, and the need to achieve and maintain it
- *intrinsic interest, pleasure, relevance or challenge* of the task
- *group dynamic:* is it competitive, collaborative, or individualistic?
- *teacher's attitudes*, e.g. what expectations does the teacher project about the learners' likelihood of success?

As the last point suggests, teachers can play a key role in motivating learners, not just in terms of choosing activities that are intrinsically motivating, but in the attitudes they project. Two researchers on motivation offer the following advice for teachers:

Ten commandments for motivating language learners

1. Set a personal example with your own behavior.
2. Create a pleasant, relaxed atmosphere in the classroom.
3. Present the tasks properly.
4. Develop a good relationship with the learners.
5. Increase the learner's linguistic self-confidence.
6. Make the language classes interesting.
7. Promote learner autonomy.
8. Personalize the learning process.
9. Increase the learners' goal-orientedness.
10. Familiarize learners with the target language culture.

noticing *SLA*

If you notice a feature of the language that you are exposed to, it attracts your attention and you make a mental note of it. For example, a learner might notice (without necessarily understanding) the sign *Mind the gap*, repeated several times on a railroad station platform. That same day, the learner hears the teacher say *would you mind* in the context of making a request in class. A day or two later, the same learner hears someone else say *I don't mind*. Each successive "noticing" both primes the learner to notice new occurrences of *mind*, and at the same time contributes to a growing understanding of the use and meaning of *mind*. Proponents of **cognitive learning theory** believe that noticing is a prerequisite for learning: without it input would remain as mere "noise". The *noticing hypothesis*, then, claims that noticing is a necessary condition for acquisition, although not the only one. Some kind of mental processing of what has been noticed is also necessary before the **input** becomes *intake*, i.e. before it is moved into long-term **memory**.

Teachers obviously play an important role in helping learners to notice features of the language. They do this when they repeat words or structures, write them on the board, or even drill them. One way of increasing the chance of learners' noticing an item is to include it lots of times in a text, a technique called *input flood*. For example, learners read a text with the word *mind* included several times. They then categorize these examples according to their meaning. A set of **concordance** lines for a particular word can be used in the same way.

There is another type of noticing, called *noticing the gap*. This is when learners are made aware of a gap in their language knowledge. This might happen when they do a **dictation**, for example. When they compare their version with the correct version, they may notice certain differences, such as the lack of past tense endings, that represent a gap in their **interlanguage**. It has been argued that noticing the gap can trigger the **restructuring** of interlanguage. That is, "minding the gap" leads learners to "fill the gap".

personalization *methodology*

When you personalize language you use it to talk about your knowledge, experience and feelings. Personalization of the type *Now write five true sentences about yourself using "used to"* is often motivated by the need to provide further practice of pre-taught grammar structures. But it is also good preparation for the kinds of situations of genuine language use that learners might encounter outside the classroom. These advantages are lost, though, if the teacher's response is to treat the exercise as *only* an exercise, and correct the learners' errors without responding to the content.

The influence of **humanistic approaches** has given a fresh impetus to personalization, both in terms of providing a more coherent rationale and suggesting a broader range of activity types. For a start (it is argued), personalization creates better classroom **dynamics**. This is because groups are more likely to form and bond if the individuals in them know more about one another. And the mental and emotional effort that is involved in finding personal associations with a language item is likely to make that item more memorable. This quality is called cognitive and affective *depth*. Finally, lessons are likely to be more interesting, and hence more motivating, if at least some of the content concerns the people in the room, rather than the characters in course books. On these grounds, some writers have suggested that personalization should not be considered simply as an "add-on", but should be the principle on which most, if not all, classroom content should be based. One teaching approach that is committed to this view is **community language learning**. In this approach, all the content of the lesson comes from the learners themselves. Personalization is not without risks, though. Teachers need to be sensitive to learner resistance: learners should have the right to "pass" on questions that they consider too intrusive. And teachers should be authentic in the way that they respond to learners' personalizations. This means that they should respond to what their learners are saying, not just how they say it.

practice *methodology*

If you practice a skill, you experience doing it a number of times in order to gain control of it. The idea that "practice makes perfect" is fundamental to **cognitive learning theory**. It is through practice that the skill becomes automatic. **Sociocultural learning theory** finds room for practice too. Performing a skill with the assistance of someone who is good at it can help in the **appropriation** of the skill. At issue, then, is not so much whether practice is beneficial, but what form it should take, when, and how much of it is necessary. In addressing these questions, it is customary to distinguish between different kinds of practice, such as *controlled practice* vs *free practice, mechanical practice* vs *meaningful/communicative practice*, and *receptive practice* vs *productive practice*.

Controlled practice is associated with the second P of the **PPP** instructional model. Practice can be controlled in at least two senses: *language control* and *interactional control*. In the first, the language that is being practiced is restricted to what has just been presented (hence it is also called *restricted practice*). For example, if the first **conditional** has been presented, learners practice this, and only this, structure, and in a repetitive way, e.g. through a sequence of **drills**. Practice is also said to be controlled if the learners' participation is overtly managed and monitored by the teacher, such as in open-class work, as opposed to closed **pairwork** or **groupwork**. One reason for this degree of control is that it maintains a focus on accuracy, and pre-empts or corrects errors. *Free practice*, on the other hand, allows learners a measure of creativity, and the opportunity to integrate the new item into their existing language "pool". It is also less controlled in terms of the interactions, with pairwork and groupwork being favored. Typical free practice activities might be **games**, **discussions** or **drama**-based activities.

Mechanical practice is a form of controlled practice, where the focus is less on the meaning of an item than on manipulating its component parts. Mechanical practice can be either oral or written: many traditional **exercises** are mechanical in this sense, such as when learners transform sentences from active into passive, or from direct speech into reported speech. The arguments in favor of controlled and mechanical practice have lost their force since the decline of **behaviorism** and its belief that learning is simply habit-formation.

Meaningful practice requires learners to display some understanding of what the item that they are practicing actually means. One way of doing this is through **personalization**. *Communicative practice* involves the learners interacting in order to complete some kind of task, such as in an *information gap activity* (➜ **communicative activity**). Proponents of a communicative approach argue that it is only this kind of practice that is truly effective. This is because learners are not simply practicing language, but are practicing the behaviors associated with the language, and this is a pre-condition for long-term behavioral change.

Finally, some practice activities are purely *receptive*. They involve the learners in identifying, selecting, or discriminating between language items, but not actually producing them. Many **consciousness-raising** activities are receptive, on the grounds that learners first need to understand a new structure before they can properly internalize it. Receptive practice is also associated with comprehension-based approaches to teaching. *Productive practice*, on the other hand, requires learners to produce the targeted items (either orally or in writing), and is associated with output-based models of learning.

There is fairly general agreement nowadays that the most effective practice activity combines at least some of the following features:

- It is meaningful, which may mean that is personalized.
- It is communicative, thus it will require learners to interact.
- It involves a degree of repetition—not of the mindless type associated with imitation drills, but of the type associated with many games.
- It is language-rich, i.e., learners have to interpret or produce a lot of language.
- Learners can be creative and take risks, but support is at hand if they need it.
- Learners are pushed, at least some of the time, to the limits of their competence
- Learners get **feedback.**

pronunciation teaching
phonology

Pronunciation is the general term for that part of language classes and courses that deals with aspects of the **phonology** of English. This includes the individual sounds (**phonemes**) of English, sounds in **connected speech**, word and sentence **stress**, **rhythm** and **intonation**. These components are customarily divided into two groups: the *segmental* features of pronunciation, i.e., the individual sounds and the way they combine, and the *suprasegmental* features, i.e., stress, rhythm and intonation. **Paralinguistic** features of speech production such as voice quality, tempo and loudness, are also classed as suprasegmental.

Effective pronunciation teaching needs to consider what goals, course design and methodology are most appropriate for the learners in question. The goal of acquiring a native-like **accent** is generally thought to be unachievable for most learners (and perhaps even undesirable). Instead, the goal of **intelligibility** is nowadays considered more realistic, if less easily measurable. It is often claimed that suprasegmental features play a greater role in intelligibility than do segmental ones. Unfortunately, however, some of these suprasegmental features, such as intonation, are considered by many teachers to be unteachable. Moreover, learners intending to interact with native speakers may need to set different goals from those learners whose purpose is to learn **English as an international language (EIL)**. For this latter group, the so-called **phonological core** is a checklist of those pronunciation features considered critical for intelligibility in EIL.

In terms of the design of course content, a basic choice is whether the pronunciation focus is *integrated* or *segregated*. In an integrated approach, pronunciation is dealt with as part of the teaching of grammar and vocabulary, or of speaking and listening. In a segregated approach it is treated in isolation. A classical segregated exercise is the **minimal pairs** task, in which learners are taught to discriminate and produce two contrasted phonemes (as in *hit* and *heat*). There are doubts as to whether this item-by-item approach to pronunciation reflects the way that the features of pronunciation are interconnected. Nor does it reflect the way that they jointly emerge over time ("as a photo emerges in the darkroom"). A related issue is whether pronunciation teaching should be *pre-emptive* or *reactive*. That is to say, should pronunciation teaching be planned around a syllabus of pre-selected items, or should the focus on pronunciation emerge *out of* practice activities, in the form, for example, of **correction**? There is evidence that the latter approach is more effective than the former.

In 1964 the writer (and former language teacher) Anthony Burgess wrote, "Nothing is more important than to acquire a set of foreign phonemes that shall be entirely acceptable to your hosts." However, there is generally less emphasis given to pronunciation teaching nowadays. Indeed, some teachers are sceptical as to the value of teaching pronunciation at all. This view is reinforced by research that suggests that the best predictors of intelligible pronunciation are "having a good ear" and prolonged residence in an English-speaking country. On the other hand, faulty pronunciation is one of the most common causes of misunderstandings. This is an argument for demanding higher standards than the learners can realistically achieve, in the hope that they will meet you "halfway."

reading *methodology*

Reading is a receptive **skill**. But the fact that it is receptive does not mean that it is passive: reading is an active, even interactive, process. Readers bring their own questions to the text, which are based on their background knowledge, and they use these to interrogate the text, modifying their questions and coming up with new ones according to the answers they get. In order to do this, they draw on a range of knowledge bases. They need to be able to decode the letters, words and grammatical structures of the individual sentences—what is called *bottom-up processing*. But they also enlist *top-down processes*, such as drawing on **discourse** and schematic knowledge, as well as on immediate contextual information. Discourse knowledge is knowing how different text-types—such as news reports, recipes or academic papers—are organized. Schematic knowledge is the reader's existing knowledge of the topic. Reading involves an interaction between these different "levels" of knowledge, where knowledge at one "level" can compensate for lack of knowledge at another.

Readers also bring their own *purposes* to texts, and these in turn determine the way they go about reading a text. The two main purposes for reading are for *information* (such as when consulting a directory), and for *pleasure* (such as when reading a novel), although these purposes may overlap. Different ways of reading include:

- *skimming (skim-reading, reading for gist)*: rapidly reading a text in order to get the *gist*, or the main ideas or sense of a text. For example, a reader might skim a film review in order to see if the reviewer liked the film or not.
- *scanning:* reading a text in search of specific information, and ignoring everything else, such as when consulting a bus timetable for a particular time and destination.
- *detailed reading:* reading a text in order to extract the maximum detail from it, such as when following the instructions for installing a household appliance.
- *reading aloud:* such as when reading a prepared speech or lecture, or reading a story aloud, or an extract from the newspaper.

A reader's purpose usually matches the writer's intentions for the text. Readers seldom read telephone books from cover to cover, for example. Nor do they normally skim through a novel looking for names beginning with *Vron* ... In classrooms, however, texts are frequently used for purposes other than those for which they were originally intended. They are often used not so much as vehicles of information or of pleasure, but as "linguistic objects," that is, as contexts for the study of features of the language. A distinction needs to be made, therefore, between two types of classroom reading: reading as *skills development*, and reading as *language study*. There is no reason why the same text cannot be used for both purposes.

Another distinction that is often made is between *intensive reading* and *extensive reading*. The former applies to the way short texts are subject to close and detailed classroom study. Extensive reading, on the other hand, means the more leisurely reading of longer texts, primarily for pleasure, or in order to accumulate vocabulary, or simply to develop sound habits of reading. This is typically done outside class, using graded **readers**, authentic texts, or literary texts.

A third important distinction is between testing reading and teaching reading. Traditional reading tasks usually involve reading a text and then answering **comprehension questions** about it. This is the testing approach. A teaching approach, on the other hand, aims to help learners to become more effective readers by training them in the *sub-skills* of reading, and by teaching them *reading strategies*. Some of the sub-skills of reading are:

- understanding words and identifying their grammatical function
- recognizing grammar features, such as word endings, and "unpacking" (or **parsing**) the syntax of sentences

- identifying the topic of the text, and recognizing topic changes
- identifying text type, text purpose, and text organization, and identifying and understanding **discourse markers** and other cohesive devices
- distinguishing key information from less important information
- identifying and understanding the gist
- inferring the writer's attitude
- following the development of an argument
- following the sequence of a narrative
- paraphrasing the text

Activities designed to develop these sub-skills include: underlining topic-related words; contrasting different text-types; comparing different examples of the same text type and identifying *generic* features; circling and categorizing discourse markers; identifying what the pronouns refer to; predicting the direction the text will take at each discourse marker; choosing the best summary of a text; putting a set of pictures in order; extracting key information on to a grid, writing a summary of the text, etc. *Strategy training* involves training learners in ways of overcoming problems when they are reading. Some useful strategies include:

- using contextual and extra-linguistic information (such as pictures, layout, headlines) to make predictions regarding what the text is about
- brainstorming background (or schematic) knowledge in advance of reading
- skimming a text in advance of a more detailed reading
- keeping the purpose of the text in mind
- guessing the meaning of words from context
- using the dictionary

There is some argument, however, as to the value of a "skills and strategies" approach to teaching reading. Most adult learners of English come to English texts with already well-developed reading skills in their own language. They already know how to skim, scan, use context clues, enlist background knowledge, and so on. Theoretically, at least, these skills are transferable. What makes reading difficult is not so much lack of reading skills as lack of *language knowledge*. That is, learners lack sufficient vocabulary and grammar to unpack sentences, and they cannot easily identify the ways that sentences are connected. This can result in "tunnel vision," with readers becoming distracted by unfamiliar words, at the expense of working out meaning from context. On the other hand, it can also result in an over-reliance on guesswork, and on superficial "text attack" strategies such as skimming. This suggests that texts need to be chosen in a way that do not over-stretch learners' ability to read them fluently. At the same time, texts should not be so easy that learners can process them simply by skimming. It also means that tasks need to be chosen so that they both match the original purpose of the text, and encourage learners to transfer their first language reading skills. Such tasks are likely to be those that motivate learners to want to read the text. This might mean activating interest in the topic of the text, through, for example, a pre-reading quiz. At the same time, classroom reading texts should be exploited, not just for their potential in developing reading skills, but as sources of language input. This will involve, at some point, detailed study of the text's formal features, such as its linking devices, its collocations or its grammar.

speaking *methodology*

Speaking is generally thought to be the most important of the four **skills**. The ability to speak a second language is often equated with proficiency in the language, as in *She speaks excellent French*. Indeed, one frustration commonly voiced by learners is that they have spent years studying English, but still can't speak it. One of the main difficulties, of course, is that speaking usually takes place spontaneously and in real time, which means that planning and production overlap. If too much **attention** is paid to planning, production suffers, and the effect is a loss of **fluency**. On the other hand, if the speaker's attention is directed solely on production, it is likely that **accuracy** will suffer, which could prejudice **intelligibility**. In order to free up attention, therefore, the speaker needs to have achieved a degree of **automaticity** in both planning and production. One way of doing this is to use memorized routines, such as **formulaic language**. Another is to use *production strategies*, such as the use of **pause fillers**, in order to "buy" planning time. The situation is complicated by the fact that most speaking is interactive. Speakers are jointly having to manage the flow of talk. The management of interaction involves *turn-taking skills*, such as knowing how and when to take, keep, and relinquish speaker turns, and also knowing how to repair misunderstandings. For language learners these processing demands are magnified through lack of basic knowledge of grammar and vocabulary. For the purposes of most day-to-day talk, however, the grammar that is required is not as complex nor need be as accurate as the grammar that is required for writing. Nor do speakers need an enormous vocabulary, especially if they have developed some **communication strategies** for getting round gaps in their knowledge. A core vocabulary of 1000–1500 high-frequency words and expressions will provide most learners with a solid basis for speaking.

Activating this knowledge, though, requires **practice**. This in turn suggests that the more speaking practice opportunities that learners are given, and the sooner, the easier speaking will become. Speaking practice means more than simply answering the teacher's questions, or repeating sentences, as in grammar practice activities. It means interacting with other speakers, sustaining long turns of talk, speaking spontaneously, and speaking about topics of the learners' choice.

Approaches to teaching speaking vary. Traditionally, speaking was considered to be a by-product of teaching grammar and vocabulary, reinforced with work on **pronunciation**. This view has been replaced by approaches that treat speaking as a skill in its own right. One such approach is to break down the speaking skill into a number of discrete sub-skills, such as *opening and closing conversations, turn-taking, repairing, paraphrasing, interrupting,* etc. Another approach is to focus on the different purposes of speaking and their associated **genres**, such as *narrating, obtaining service, giving a presentation, making small talk*, etc. This approach is particularly well suited to learners who have a specific purpose for learning English. A third is to adopt a topic-based approach, where learners are encouraged to speak freely on a range of topics, at least some of which they have chosen themselves. This is the format used in many conversation classes. Typical activity types for the teaching of speaking include: **dialogues**, **drama** activities (including *roleplays* and *simulations*), games, discussions and debates, as well as informal classroom chat.

task *methodology*

A task is a classroom activity whose focus is on communicating meaning. The objective of a task may be to reach some consensus on an issue, to solve a problem, to draft a plan, to design something, or to persuade someone to do something. In contrast, practicing a preselected item of language (such as the present perfect) for its own sake would not be a valid task objective. In the performance of the task, learners are expected to make use of their own language resources. In theory, tasks may be receptive or productive, and may be done individually or in pairs or small groups. However, in practice, most activities that are labelled "tasks" in coursebooks involve production (either speaking or writing, or both) and require learners to interact with one another.

Tasks are the organizing principle in **task-based learning.** In order to devise a syllabus of tasks it is necessary both to classify tasks, and to identify the factors that make one task more difficult than another. Different criteria for classifying tasks have been suggested. For example, tasks can be *open-ended* or *closed*. An open-ended task is one in which learners know there is no predetermined solution. It might be planning an excursion, or debating a topical issue. A closed task, on the other hand, requires learners to discover the solution to a problem, such as identifying the differences in a *spot-the-difference* task (➜ **communicative activity**). Tasks can also be classified according to the kinds of operations they involve, such as *ranking, selecting, sorting, comparing, surveying* and *problem-solving*.

Factors which influence the degree of difficulty of the task, and hence which affect the grading of tasks, include:

- *linguistic factors:* How complex is the language that learners will need to draw on, in order to do the task? How much help, either before, or during the task, will they get with their language needs?
- *cognitive factors:* Does the task require the processing of complex data? Is the task type familiar to learners?
- *performance factors:* Do the learners have to interact in real time in order to do the task? Do they have time to rehearse? Do they have to "go public"?

The term *task* is now widely accepted as a useful way of labeling certain types of classroom activity, including many which have a thinly disguised grammar agenda. But the concept of task is not without its critics. Some writers feel that the associations of task with "work" undervalues the more playful–and possibly less authentic or communicative–types of classroom activity, such as games, songs and drama.

vocabulary teaching *methodology*

Vocabulary describes that area of language learning that is concerned with word knowledge. Vocabulary learning is a major goal in most teaching programs. It hasn't always been so. In methods such as **audiolingualism**, vocabulary was subordinated to the teaching of grammar structures. Words were simply there to fill the slots in the sentence patterns. The move towards *semantic* (i.e., meaning-based) **syllabuses** in the 1970s, along with the use of **authentic** materials, saw a revival of interest in vocabulary teaching. Subsequently, developments in **corpus** linguistics and **discourse analysis** started to blur the distinction between vocabulary and grammar. In the 1990s the **lexical approach** ushered in a major re-think regarding the role of vocabulary. This concerned both the *selection* of items (**frequency** being a deciding factor) and the type of items: **formulaic language** (or lexical chunks) were recognized as being essential for both **fluency** and **idiomaticity**. These developments have influenced the design of teaching materials. Most contemporary coursebooks incorporate a lexical syllabus alongside the grammar one. Recent developments in lexicography have complemented this trend. There is now a wide range of **dictionaries** available for learners, many of which come with sophisticated software for accessing databases of examples and collocations.

It is now generally agreed that, in terms of goals, learners need a receptive vocabulary of around 3000 high-frequency words (or, better, **word families**) in order to achieve independent user status. This will give them around ninety per cent coverage of normal text. For a productive vocabulary, especially for speaking, they may only need half this number.

Classroom approaches to achieving these goals include dedicated vocabulary lessons. Typically these take the form of teaching *lexical sets* of words (i.e., groups of thematically linked words) using a variety of means, including visual **aids**, demonstration, situations, texts, and dictionary work. As well as the **meaning** of the items, the **form**, both spoken (ie, **pronunciation**) and written (ie, **spelling**), needs to be dealt with, especially if the words are being taught for productive use. Other aspects of word knowledge that may need to be highlighted include **connotation** and **style**, **collocation**, derived forms, and grammatical features, such as the word's **word class**. Vocabulary is also taught as preparation for listening or reading (*pre-teaching vocabulary*) or as a by-product of these skills.

It would be impossible, in class, to teach all the words that learners need. Learners therefore need opportunities for *incidental* learning, e.g. through *extensive reading*. They may also benefit from training in how to make the most of these opportunities, e.g. by means of dictionary use, note-keeping, etc. Some strategies for deducing the meaning of unfamiliar words will also help.

Amassing a fully-functioning vocabulary is essentially a **memory** task, and techniques to help in the memorizing of words can be usefully taught, too. It also helps to provide learners with repeated encounters with new words, e.g. through the re-reading of texts, or by reading several texts about the same topic. Constant recycling of newly learned words is essential. One simple way of doing this is to have a *word box* (or word bag) in the classroom. New words are written on to small cards and added to the word box. At the beginning of the next lesson, these words can be used as the basis for a review activity. For example, the teacher can take words out of the box and ask learners to define them, provide a translation or put them into a sentence. The words can also form the basis for peer-testing activities, in which learners take a number of word cards and test each other in pairs or small groups.

writing *methodology*

Like speaking, writing is a productive **skill**, and, like other skills, writing involves a hierarchy of *subskills*. These range from the most mechanical (such as handwriting or typing legibly) through to the ability to organize the written text and lay it out according to the conventions of the particular text type. Along the way, writers also need to be able to:

- produce grammatically accurate sentences
- connect and punctuate these sentences
- select and maintain an appropriate style
- signal the direction that the message is taking
- anticipate the reader's likely questions so as to be able to structure the message accordingly

In order to enable these skills, writers need an extensive knowledge base, not only at the level of vocabulary and grammar, but at the level of connected discourse. This includes familiarity with a range of different text types, such as *informal letters*, *instructions*, *product descriptions*, etc. It follows that if classroom writing is mainly spelling- or grammar-focused, many of the sub-skills of writing will be neglected.

Nevertheless, the teaching of writing has tended to focus on the "lower-level" features of the skill, such as being able to write sentences that are both accurate and complex, that demonstrate internal cohesion, and that are connected to the sentences next to them. This language-based approach is justified on the grounds that stricter standards of accuracy are usually required in writing than in speaking. Also, writing demands a greater degree of explicitness than speaking, since writers and their readers are separated in time and space. They therefore can't rely on immediate feedback in order to clear up misunderstandings.

By contrast, a text-based approach to teaching writing takes a more "top-down" view. This approach finds support in **discourse analysis**, which shows that a **text** is more than a series of sentences, however neatly linked. Instead, texts are organized according to larger *macrostructures*, such as problem-solution, or definition-examples. Hence, learners need explicit guidance in how texts are structured. This typically involves analyzing and imitating models of particular text types. For example, a business letter might be analyzed in terms of its overall layout, the purpose of each of its paragraphs, the grammatical and lexical choices within each paragraph, and the punctuation. Each of these features is then practiced in isolation. They are then recombined in tasks aimed first at reproducing the original text and then at producing similar texts incorporating different content.

This approach is called a *product approach* to the teaching of writing, since the focus is exclusively on producing a text (the product) that reproduces the model. By contrast, a *process approach* argues that writers do not in fact start with a clear idea of the finished product. Rather, the text emerges out of a creative process. This process includes: *planning (generating ideas, goal setting* and *organizing), drafting* and *re-drafting; reviewing*, including *editing* and *proofreading*, and, finally, *"publishing"*. Advocates of a process approach argue for a more organic sequence of classroom activities, beginning with the brainstorming of ideas, writing preliminary drafts, comparing drafts, re-drafting, and *conferencing*, that is, talking through their draft with the teacher, in order to fine-tune their ideas.

The process approach to writing has a lot in common with the **communicative approach** to language teaching, and each has drawn support from the other. The communicative approach views writing as an act of communication in which the writer interacts with a reader or readers for a particular purpose. The purpose might be to ask for information about a language course, to relay personal news, to complain about being overcharged at a hotel, or simply to entertain and amuse. Thus, advocates of a communicative approach argue that classroom writing tasks should be motivated by a clear purpose and that writers should have their reader(s) in mind at all stages of the writing process. Such principles are now reflected in the design of writing tasks in public examinations, such as this one, from the Cambridge ESOL First Certificate in English (FCE) paper:

> The school where you learn English has decided to buy some videos in English. You have been asked to write a report to the Principal, suggesting what kinds of videos the school should buy. In your report you should also explain why students at the school will like these videos.
> Write your report.

The social purposes of writing are also foregrounded by proponents of a *genre-based approach*. **Genre** analysis attempts to show how the structure of particular text types are shaped by the purposes they serve in specific social and cultural contexts. Put simply, a business letter is the way it is because of what it does. Advocates of genre-based teaching reject a process approach to teaching writing. They argue that to emphasize self-expression at the expense of teaching the generic structures of texts may in fact disempower learners. Many learners, especially those who are learning English as a *second* language, need a command of those genres—such as writing a resume, or requesting a bank loan—that permit access to the host community. A genre approach to teaching writing is not unlike a product approach, therefore. It starts with model texts that are subjected to analysis and replication. The difference is that these models are closely associated with their contexts of use, and they are analyzed in functional terms as much as in linguistic ones. The genre approach has been particularly influential in the teaching of academic writing.

In reality, none of these approaches is entirely incompatible with any other. Resourceful teachers tend to blend elements of each. For example, they may encourage learners to "discover" what they want to write, using a process approach. They may then give them a model text, both as a source of useful language items, and as a template for the final product. They may also provide exercises in specific sub-skills, such as linking sentences, or using a formal style.

Life Skills

What are Life Skills?

Life Skills are the skills students need to deal effectively with the challenges in everyday life, whether at school, at work or in their personal lives. Students who are able to understand and use these skills, along with their educational qualifications, will be better placed to take advantage of educational and employment opportunities. In a constantly changing environment, having life skills is an essential part of being able to meet the challenges of everyday life. The dramatic changes in global economies over the past five years have been matched with the transformation in technology and these are all impacting on education, the workplace and our home life. To cope with the increasing pace and change of modern life, students need new life skills such as the ability to deal with stress and frustration. Today's students will have many new jobs over the course of their lives, with associated pressures and the need for flexibility. As medical science advances, home life and the community will place additional demands on future generations.

(*Life Skills Handbook* page 2)

Topics:

- Social Skills
- People Management
- Critical Thinking
- Time Management
- Cultural Awareness
- Networking
- Career and Work
- Study Skills
- Creativity
- Self-awareness
- Getting Organized

(www.macmillanenglish.com/life-skills/classroom-resources/)

How do we approach Life Skills in this book?

In every unit of *American Inside Out Evolution* one of these topics will be discussed, according to the theme of the unit, and students will have the opportunity to reflect and discuss based on simple activities.

MACMILLAN LIFE SKILLS

The Common European Framework of Reference for Language Learning

Introduction

The Common European Framework of Reference (CEFR) is a widely used standard created by the Council of Europe. In the classroom, familiarity with the CEFR can be of great help to any teacher in identifying students' actual progress and helping them to set their learning priorities.

Students can use the descriptors (description of competences) at any point to get a detailed, articulated, and personal picture of their own individual progress. This is important, as no two language learners progress in the same way, and consequently it is always rather artificial to apply a "framework level" to a class as a whole, or to a course or course book.

The European Language Portfolio is another Council of Europe project, designed to give every learner a structure for keeping a record of their language learning experiences and their progress as described in the CEFR. Up-to-date information about developments with the CEFR and Portfolio can be found on www.coe.int/portfolio.

The Swiss-based Eurocentres Foundation played a major role in the development of the levels and the descriptors for the CEFR and the prototype Portfolio. The CEFR descriptors, developed in a Swiss National Research Foundation project, were presented in clearer, simpler, self-assessment form in the prototype (Swiss) Portfolio. There are now dozens of different national versions of the Portfolio for different educational sectors, but the only version for adults is that developed from the Swiss version[1] by EAQUALS[2] (European Association for Quality Language Services) in collaboration with ALTE[3] (Association of Language Testers in Europe). The descriptors used in this guide are taken from the EAQUALS/ ALTE Portfolio. An electronic version that can be completed on-line can be downloaded in English or French from www.eelp.org. The EAQUALS/ ALTE portfolio descriptors have been used in this guide, as they are more concrete and practical than the original CEFR descriptors.

CEFR Checklists

This Beginner level is appropriate for students who have had no previous contact with the language, or whose knowledge of the language is very sketchy. By the end of the Beginner level, if the students have had access to English outside the classroom, and have had the opportunity to practice, they should be able to do most of the things described at the A1 level.

In order to help the teacher and student assess their progress, we have provided a list of the A1 descriptors for each unit of the Beginner level. So, for example, in Unit 1 nearly all of the descriptors listed are things that the students certainly won't feel confident about doing yet. However, with a lot of help and support from the teacher, many of the students should be feeling that they can try to do a range of things in English by the end of the unit. Once they have studied more units, they should begin to feel more confident about certain aspects of the language. The descriptors in these charts allow the teacher to see a typical pattern of language acquisition.

At beginner level, students will need the help of the teacher if they are to use the self-assessment at all, since they won't be able to understand the descriptors. The descriptors may be of use to the teacher; not in formally assessing the students, but in gauging their progress through the course across the whole range of language abilities. This will help clarify for the teacher which students are making quicker or slower progress in the different areas, and will assist them in planning the focus of future lessons.

The CEFR can be used to follow student progress. By checking whether the students' confidence is at an appropriate level across the whole range of language skills at any point in the course, the teacher can decide if there is an area that requires more practice.

---

1 Schneider, Gunther, & North, Brian (2000): "Fremdsprachen konnen – was heisst das?"
Zirrich, Ruegger North, Brian (2000): "The Development of a Common Framework Scale of Language Proficiency", New York, Peter Lang.

2 EAQUALS is a pan-European language school accreditation body with over 100 full members.

3 ALTE is an association dedicated to raising standards in language testing and encompasses the major European examination providers. Eurocentres provides high quality language teaching in countries where the language concerned is spoken. EAQUALS, ALTE and Eurocentres are the three NGOS advisers for language learning to the Council of Europe and all three implement the CEFR.

CEFR Student Checklists

Unit 1

Complete the checklist.

1 = I can do this with a lot of help from my teacher.
2 = I can do this with a little help.
3 = I can do this fairly well.
4 = I can do this really well.
5 = I can do this almost perfectly.

Competences	Page	Your score
I can introduce myself and use basic greeting and leave-taking expressions.	10, 14	1 2 3 4 5
I can understand simple personal questions when people speak slowly and clearly.	10, 14	1 2 3 4 5
I can understand 1-10 and telephone numbers.	11, 15	1 2 3 4 5
I can understand a questionnaire (entry permit form, hotel registration form) well enough to give the most important information about myself (name, last name, date of birth, nationality).	11	1 2 3 4 5
I can understand when someone speaks very slowly to me and articulates carefully, with long pauses for me to assimilate meaning.	14	1 2 3 4 5
I can very simply ask somebody to repeat what they said.	14	1 2 3 4 5

Unit 2

Complete the checklist.

1 = I can do this with a lot of help from my teacher.
2 = I can do this with a little help.
3 = I can do this fairly well.
4 = I can do this really well.
5 = I can do this almost perfectly.

Competences	Page	Your score
I can understand information about people (place of residence, age, nationality, etc.) in simple conversations.	16, 17	1 2 3 4 5
I can ask people questions about where they live, people they know, things they have, etc. and answer such questions addressed to me provided they are articulated slowly and clearly.	16, 17, 54, 56	1 2 3 4 5
I can understand numbers 1-100 and prices.	18, 19, 21	1 2 3 4 5
I can handle numbers, quantities and cost.	18, 19, 20, 21	1 2 3 4 5

Unit 3

Complete the checklist.

1 = I can do this with a lot of help from my teacher.
2 = I can do this with a little help.
3 = I can do this fairly well.
4 = I can do this really well.
5 = I can do this almost perfectly.

Competences	Page	Your score
I can understand simple information and questions about family and people.	22, 23	1 2 3 4 5
I can understand short simple texts on everyday topics, for example, family.	24	1 2 3 4 5
I can talk about myself simply, for example, my possessions and my family.	25	1 2 3 4 5
I can write sentences and simple phrases about myself or other people on basic everyday topics, for example, family and home.	25	1 2 3 4 5
I can understand when someone speaks very slowly to me and use an appropriate response to show interest	26	1 2 3 4 5
I can introduce somebody and use basic greeting and leave-taking expressions.	26	1 2 3 4 5

Unit 4

Complete the checklist.

1 = I can do this with a lot of help from my teacher.
2 = I can do this with a little help.
3 = I can do this fairly well.
4 = I can do this really well.
5 = I can do this almost perfectly.

Competences	Page	Your score
I can write sentences and simple phrases about myself, for example where I live and what I do.	32	1 2 3 4 5
I can ask people questions about where they live, people they know, their possessions, job, interests, routines, etc. and answer such questions addressed to me provided they are articulated slowly and clearly.	32, 33, 55, 57	1 2 3 4 5
I can understand short simple texts on everyday topics, for example, daily routine.	34	1 2 3 4 5
I can understand and indicate time, for example, days of the week and time of day.	33, 35	1 2 3 4 5
I can have a simple phone conversation.	36	1 2 3 4 5
I can write a daily schedule and talk about my routine.	36	1 2 3 4 5

Unit 5

Complete the checklist.

1 = I can do this with a lot of help from my teacher.
2 = I can do this with a little help.
3 = I can do this fairly well.
4 = I can do this really well.
5 = I can do this almost perfectly.

Competences	Page	Your score
I can write a short description of where I live and work.	39, 40	1 2 3 4 5
I can describe where I live and work; ask and answer simple questions about city attractions and places in town.	41, 42	1 2 3 4 5
I can understand questions and instructions addressed carefully and slowly to me and follow, short, simple directions.	42	1 2 3 4 5
I can make simple recommendations about things to see and places to visit.	42	1 2 3 4 5

Unit 6

Complete the checklist.

1 = I can do this with a lot of help from my teacher.
2 = I can do this with a little help.
3 = I can do this fairly well.
4 = I can do this really well.
5 = I can do this almost perfectly.

Competences	Page	Your score
I can identify people from a simple description of their clothes.	44	1 2 3 4 5
I can extract specific information from short, simple texts on everyday topics, for example, clothes.	45	1 2 3 4 5
I can describe what I and other people are wearing and doing in pictures or at the time of speaking.	46	1 2 3 4 5
I can understand simple conversations about what people are doing.	46	1 2 3 4 5
I can ask and answer simple questions, initiate and respond to simple statements in areas of immediate need or on very familiar topics.	47	1 2 3 4 5
I can talk about everyday habits using frequency adverbs, for example, *always, sometimes, never*.	47, 48	1 2 3 4 5
I can make simple purchases where pointing or other gestures can support what I say.	48	1 2 3 4 5

0 Instructions *Teacher's notes*

This introductory unit equips students with some basic language for following spoken and written classroom instructions. The exercises are simple, asking the students just to listen and repeat or follow a simple instruction.

1 ▶ 2

Focus the students' attention on the picture and give them a minute or two to look at it. Students are going to listen to the words below the picture and repeat them after the speaker. Play the recording. When the students have repeated the words as a class, you could ask for individual repetition of the words.

Extra activity

You could give further practice by saying the words and getting the students to mime the actions. i.e. Point: students point. Listen: students exaggerate listening by cupping their hand over their ear. You could then get the students to do this in pairs.

2 ▶ 3

This is another listen and repeat exercise, but this time all the instructions are full sentences rather than individual words. Focus the students' attention on the pictures and read the captions with the class. Make sure everyone understands all the instructions by getting students to mime the actions. Then play the recording and ask the students to repeat each sentence after the speaker. Do this chorally at first and then get individual students to say the instructions. Again, you could get students to mime the actions.

3 ▶ 4

This exercise introduces some more basic instructions. Illustrate the meaning of each of the words by doing the action on the board, i.e. you write *Hello. My name's* ______ on the board and then you pause and say *Complete* before completing the sentence with your name. Then play the recording and ask them to listen to the instructions.

4

Now students get the chance to put the rubric instructions they have learned into practice. Begin this with the whole class. Focus the students' attention on item 1 and point out that this corresponds to item a) in Exercise 3. Ask the students to complete the sentence using their own names.

Do the same with item 2, pointing out that this corresponds to item b) in Exercise 3. Point out the other correspondences.

Then ask students to work individually to complete the exercise. Go around checking that everyone knows what to do and has fully understood all the instructions. You may need to explain the male (♂) and female (♀) symbols in item 4.

Now that your students have studied some basic classroom language in English, try to use it as much as possible in subsequent lessons. If the students look uncertain when you give an instruction in English, take them back to this unit and remind them of the meaning.

Before the next lesson

Bring in the following objects for Grammar, Exercise 2 on page 12 of the Student's Book: a bag; two or three books; some pens; some keys; a cell phone.

1D Overview

Section	Aims	What the students are doing
Grammar SB page 10	Possessive determiners: *My* and *your* *Be*: contractions	Completing short sentences with possessive determiners: *my* and *your*. Practicing the use of *be* contractions in introductions.
Speaking SB page 10	Introductions	Substituting students' own names in a simple introduction dialogue.
Grammar SB page 11	Possessive determiners: *His* and *her*	Listening and completing introductions with *his* and *her*. Asking questions about the names of other students in the class.
Vocabulary SB page 11	Numbers *0 to 10*	Listening to and repeating numbers 0 to 10. Listening to and writing down telephone numbers.
Speaking SB page 11	Names and personal information Asking for personal information	Asking questions and completing a page from an old address book with names and telephone numbers of other students.
Vocabulary SB page 12	Everyday common objects Plurals	Listening to and repeating words for common objects. Identifying common objects.
Grammar SB page 12	*This* and *these*	Asking questions and identifying objects. Asking questions with *this* and *these*.
Listening SB page 13	Listening for specific details	Listening to a conversation and checking the things the speakers have.
Pronunciation SB page 13	The alphabet	Listening to and repeating the letters of the alphabet. Listening to and identifying abbreviations.
Language for Life SB page 14	Expressions for communicating Personal information	Listening to and completing conversations. Listening to and repeating expressions.
Life Skills SB page 14	Studying: materials	Choosing materials needed for English study.
Vocabulary Extra SB page 15	Everyday objects Numbers	Matching pictures with words. Dictating and writing numbers.

1 ID *Teacher's notes*

Warm-up

Introduce yourself to the class with a simple friendly greeting such as *Hello, I'm (name).* Go round and greet each of the students individually, encouraging them to respond with *Hello, I'm (Julio).*

Language note

Vocabulary: ID

ID is a shortened form of "identity" and is now widely used. For example, *Can I see some ID, please?* You pronounce the two letters separately /ˌaɪˈdi/.

Vocabulary: *name*

The phrase *My name's Bond … James Bond* has been repeated in all the James Bond movies and has achieved a kind of iconic status as the way James Bond always introduces himself. Some of your students may recognize this from having seen some of the movies. In fact, the most appropriate answer to the question *What's your name?* is usually to give your first name only. In more formal situations, students should probably give both their first name and their last name.

Grammar (SB page 10)

Possessive determiners

1

- Focus the students' attention on the picture taken from the James Bond movie *Spectre* (see Cultural Note). Then focus attention on the dialogue. Ask students to read the dialogue.
- Focus the students' attention on the use of *your* and *my*. Make sure they know the difference between them. You could then ask several pairs of students to role-play the conversation.
- Point out the information about contractions of the verb *be* in the margin. Ask students to find the contractions in the conversation they have just practiced (*What's* and *name's*).

Language notes

Grammar: possessive determiners

The possessive determiners *my, your, his, her, its, our,* and *their* are sometimes known as "possessive adjectives" in older grammars and textbooks. In this unit, only *my, your, his,* and *her* are presented. There is more work on possessive determiners in Unit 3.

Grammar: contractions

Throughout the book encourage the use of contractions because it sounds more natural. While it's grammatically correct not to use contractions, native speakers will generally do so when speaking.

Cultural note

James Bond

James Bond is a fictional British spy, code named 007. The first Bond novel, *Casino Royale,* was written by Ian Fleming in 1953. The first Bond movie, *Dr. No,* was shown in 1962. Bond has been played by six actors including Sean Connery, Roger Moore, Pierce Brosnan, and Daniel Craig.

2

- Again, focus the students' attention on the picture. Students read and complete the dialogue with *my* and *your*.
- Note the useful phrase *Nice to meet you* which completes the introduction. Ask the students to work in pairs and role-play the meeting between James Bond and Madeleine Swan. Then focus their attention on the contraction *I'm* in the dialogue.

ANSWERS:

- Hello. I'm Madeleine Swann. What's your name?
- My name's Bond … James Bond.
- Nice to meet you, James.

Speaking (SB page 10)

1 ▶ 5

- Focus the students' attention on the gaps in the dialogue. Students listen to the dialogue and complete it.

ANSWERS:

I'm, your, My, you

5

Woman:	Hello. I'm Sandra. What's your name?
Man:	Hello, Sandra. My name's Diego. Nice to meet you.

2

- Read out the conversation in the speech bubbles to the class. Then choose a confident student and demonstrate the dialogue using your own names.
- Put the students in pairs and ask them to practice the conversation using their own names. When they have finished, they can mingle around the class introducing themselves to other students. Monitor and help where necessary.
- If you like, ask the students to practice the dialogue "Bond-style": *My name's Ramirez ... Ana Ramirez.*

Grammar (SB page 11)

Possessive determiners

1 6

- Focus the students' attention on the possessive determiners *his* and *her* in the box. Point out that *his* is used for men and *her* for women. With speakers of some languages you may need to explain that the choice of adjective is governed by the gender of the owner of the object, not the object itself.
- Ask the students to look at the photo of actor Daniel Craig, who plays James Bond, and actor Naomi Harris, who plays Miss Moneypenny.
- Play the recording and ask the students to complete a) and b).

ANSWERS:

a What's his name?
His name's Daniel Craig.
b What's her name?
Her name's Naomi Harris.

Cultural note

Miss Moneypenny

In these books and movies, James Bond enjoys a flirtatious relationship with his boss's secretary, called Miss Moneypenny. In recent movies this role has been played by Naomi Harris.

2

- Read the speech bubbles with the class, and demonstrate the activity by asking questions about the names of some male and female students with one or two confident students.
- Then ask the students to mingle and ask each other about the names of the other students in the class. Monitor and help, making sure they're using *his* to ask about male students and *her* to ask about female students.

Vocabulary (SB page 11)

Numbers

1 7

- Point out the list of numbers in the box. Ask why they think the first parts of *zero* and *seven* are underlined (these are words with more than one syllable and the underlining indicates the main stress), and get them to practice saying these two words correctly. Ask them what *007* at the bottom of the list is (James Bond's secret agent number).
- Play the recording and ask the students to repeat the numbers after the speaker. When they have done this chorally, ask individual students to repeat numbers after you. Encourage students to get the intonation right when saying *zero* and *seven*.

Language notes

Vocabulary: numbers

0 is often pronounced like the letter "O" when saying numbers one figure at a time—for example, in a reference number or telephone number. Note that 0 can also be pronounced *zero*.

When a figure is repeated, we can usually say *three three*. However, James Bond (007) is always known as *Double O Seven*.

2 8

- Do the first one as an example with the class and then ask them to work in pairs to complete the rest.
- When they have finished, play the recording for them to check their answers. Then ask them to repeat the numbers after the speakers.

ANSWERS:

a three, four, five
b three, two, one
c six, eight, ten
d seven, nine

8

a one, two, three, four, five
b five, four, three, two, one
c two, four, six, eight, ten
d one, three, five, seven, nine

Extra activity

To give further practice of the numbers, do a finger dictation. Demonstrate to the students by calling out a number and holding up the corresponding number of fingers. Repeat until all the students are holding up the correct number of fingers. Then call out another number and check they are holding up the correct number of fingers again. Repeat until everyone has the correct number.

Ask a stronger or more confident student to take over your role and then give everyone a turn around the class.

3 ▶ 9

- Make sure they know the difference between a home number and a cell phone number. Demonstrate cell phone number by holding up your cell phone and saying *My cell phone number is ...* and give the first four numbers. Then play the recording and ask the students to complete the numbers they hear.

> **ANSWERS:**
>
> **a** 302-741-6995
> **b** 240-856-3213

- Check answers with the class, then go around asking a few students for their own home and cell phone numbers.

Speaking (SB page 11)

Names

- Focus the students' attention on the information in the margin and make sure they know the difference between *first name* and *last name* (sometimes also called *family name*). Demonstrate with your own first name and last name. Practice the conversation from the speech bubbles with a confident student. Get the student to ask the questions and respond with your own first name and last name.
- Focus the students' attention on the address book. With the class, make a list on the board of the questions they need to find out the missing information. Then ask the students to mingle and find two students to question. They should write the information they gather in the address book.

Vocabulary (SB page 12)

1 ▶ 10

- This exercise introduces the students to some more vocabulary: common objects. Focus attention on the picture, then play the recording. Tell them to point to the objects in the picture as they hear them, and ask them to repeat the words after the speakers. Encourage them to get the stress in the right place in *computer, camera, cell phone,* and *passport*. Remind the students that the underlining will help them get the main stress on the correct part of the word.
- Note that the words *pens*, *keys*, and *books* are plural: there are four pens, several keys, and three books in the picture. Tell them that the single objects (*bag, computer, camera,* etc.) could be made plural by the addition of an *s* at the end. Explain also that the plural words don't have the indefinite article *a* in front of them.

2 Pairwork

- Demonstrate this simple game with a confident student. Cover the list of words in your books and then say a number and get the student to identify the object in the picture that has that number. Then change roles, with the student calling out a number and you identifying the correct object.
- Put the students in pairs and encourage them to play the game. Make sure they have covered the list of words.

Grammar (SB page 12)

Nouns; *this/these*

1 ▶ 11

- Focus the students' attention on the information in the margin about the use of *this* and *these*. Get them to practice saying the two words, making sure they differentiate between the short /ɪ/ sound of *this* and the longer /i/ sound of *these*. Make sure they know that you use *this* with singular words and *these* with plurals. Also, check that they can pronounce *they're* /ðeɪr/ correctly, and that they understand that *are* is the plural form of *is*.
- Look at the first item with the whole class. Make sure they know that in the picture there's only one bag, so the question is: *What's this?* and the answer: *It's a bag*. Then ask them to go through the other items and underline the correct answers.
- Play the recording for the students to check their answers. Then play it again and ask them to repeat after the speakers.

> **ANSWERS:**
>
> **a** It's a bag.
> **b** It's a computer.
> **c** They're books.
> **d** They're pens.
> **e** They're keys.
> **f** It's a cell phone.
> **g** It's a passport.
> **h** It's a camera.

Extra activity

Take some of the items in Exercise 1 from your own bag or pocket. Ask students to identify them.

Put the things in a box at the front of the class and allow students to come up, put their hand in the box and pull out an item to ask the rest of the class about.

Language note

Vocabulary: objects from pocket

Avoid "money" which is an uncountable noun and cannot be used with this structure.

Here are some possible objects that the students might find in their pockets: *a bus ticket, a wallet, a photo, a pack of gum, ID card, coins.*

2 Grammar Extra 1

Ask the students to turn to Grammar Extra 1. Here they'll find an explanation of the grammar they've been studying and further exercises to practice it.

ANSWERS:

1
a It's a pen.
b It's a book.
c It's a computer.
d It's a bus.
e It's a passport.
f It's a dictionary.

2
a They're pens.
b They're books.
c They're computers.
d They're buses.
e They're passports.
f They're dictionaries.

3
a What's this? It's a bag.
b What are these? They're pictures.
c What's this? It's a camera.
d What's this? It's a cell phone.
e What are these? They're keys.

Language note

Vocabulary: plurals

Be careful of plural forms of some objects which students might find in their pocket or bag. For example, *watch/watches, brush/brushes, diary/diaries.*

Listening (SB page 13)

Nouns; *this/these*

1 12

- Focus the students' attention on the picture and give them time to think about the situation.
- Ask the students to look at the chart. Point out that there's a column for them to check the things that are in the woman's bag, and a column for them to check the things that are in the man's bag. There's already a check in the woman's column to show that she has a computer. Note that they'll find out what is in each bag by listening to the conversation.
- Play the recording for the students to listen and check the correct objects. You may need to play it more than once.
- Check answers with the class.

ANSWERS:

Her bag: a computer, a camera, books, a cell phone, a passport
His bag: a cell phone

12

(G = Greg; T = Tina)
G: Hey, Tina.
T: Yes, Greg.
G: What's in your bag?
T: A computer, a camera, three books, a cell phone, er...my passport.... What's in your bag?
G: A cell phone.
T: Oh. Where's your computer?
G: I don't need one. I have my phone.
T: Where's your camera?
G: I don't need one. I have my phone.
T: Where's your passport?
G: I don't nee...Passport? Oh, no!

2

Ask the students, 'What isn't in his bag?'.

ANSWERS:

a passport

Pronunciation (SB page 13)

The alphabet

1 ▶ 13

- Note how the letters of the alphabet are divided up in the table in the box. They form a kind of poem as the students will hear when they listen to the recording.
- Play the recording and ask the students to repeat the letters in the margin line by line.

Language note

Pronunciation: the alphabet

Some students confuse the pronunciation of *A* /eɪ/, *E* /i/ and *I* /aɪ/, so it's worth giving these sounds extra practice. Other letters that can cause problems are: *J* /dʒ/ and *G* /g/, and *B* /b/ and *V* /v/. It's a good idea to give extra attention to the pronunciation of the letters that cause your students most difficulties.

2 ▶ 14

- Read out the first line of letters (*B, C, D*, etc.) and tell the students that they all have the same vowel sound /i/. Point out the phonetic symbols at the beginning of the line and explain that these symbols are used in dictionaries to show how a word should be pronounced.
- Explain that the letters of the alphabet can be grouped according to their vowel sound. The letter *E* goes in this first group because it has the same sound as *B, C, D*, etc.
- Play the recording and ask the students to complete the groups with the missing letters from. the box.
- Play the recording again for them to repeat the letters

ANSWERS:

1 E
3 A
4 U
5 I
6 O

3 ▶ 15

- Explain that abbreviations are shortened forms of words. If they are formed just from the initial letters, then the letters are pronounced individually. Acronyms are words, usually made up of the initial letters of a group of words. They are pronounced as words, not as individual letters. For example, *NATO* stands for *North Atlantic Treaty Organization*.
- Play the recording and ask the students to number the abbreviations as they hear them.
- Check answers with the class and then ask them to repeat the abbreviations.
- Note that the odd one out in this list is *OK* whose letters don't actually stand for any words beginning with *O* and *K*. *OK* simply means *all right*. The others are: *CIA = Central Intelligence Agency*, *VIP = very important person*, *CNN = Cable News Network*, *UK = the United Kingdom*, *USA = the United States of America*.
- Ask the students to suggest any more abbreviations that they know. Write any ideas on the board and get the students to practice saying them aloud. Suggestions they come up with might include *BBC* (British Broadcasting Corporation) and *DJ* (disk jockey).

ANSWERS:

1 USA
2 UK
3 VIP
4 OK
5 CNN
6 CIA

Extra activity

To give further practice of the alphabet, do an alphabet dictation, spelling out words that the students have already seen in the unit. For example, *nice*, *meet*, *my*, *five*, *number*, *first*.

As you dictate, get the students to write down the letters. They should then call out the word. Finally, ask them to find examples of this word in the book.

Language note

Pronunciation: additional abbreviations

Note that acronyms are pronounced as words, for example, NATO /ˈneɪ.toʊ/, FIFA, /ˈfiːfə/ and UNICEF /ˈju.nəˌsɛf/.

Language for Life (SB page 14)

1 ▶ 16

- Focus the students' attention on the illustration which shows a male receptionist and a female student in a language school. He's taking down the student's details. Give students time to look at the illustration and think about what's happening.

- Play the recording for the students to listen and complete the conversation. You may need to play it more than once.
- Check answers with the class.

ANSWERS:

1 C-A-S-T-I-L-L-A
2 C-A-S-T-I-L-L-A
3 Castilla

▶ 16

(R = Receptionist; S = Student)
R: Welcome to The Oxford English School. What's your name?
S: Yolanda.
R: Can you spell that, please?
S: Y-O-L-A-N-D-A.
R And your last name?
S: C-A-S-T-I-L-L-A.
R: Sorry, can you repeat that, please?
S: C-A-S-T-I-L-L-A.
R: Thank you, Ms. Castilla.
S: Please call me Yolanda.
R: OK. Thank you, Yolanda.

Language note

Grammar: *can*

Can you ...? in this context is a polite request.

2 ▶ 17

- Play the recording. The students repeat the phrase after the speaker. Encourage them to match the speaker's intonation.

3 Pairwork

- Students choose one of the people from the illustrations and work together to write a new conversation, using Exercise 1 as a model. Go around, monitoring and giving help.
- When the students have finished, ask pairs to perform their conversations for the rest of the class. Encourage them, where possible, to make eye contact with each other when they say their lines, rather than simply reading them out.

4 Pairwork

- Put the students in pairs and tell them who will be Student A, and who will be Student B.
- While they're doing the exercise, go around monitoring and giving help. Take note of any errors which may need focusing on later, and also any examples of good language use which you can praise. Check answers with the class.

ANSWERS:

1 Dwayne Johnson
2 Beyoncé Knowles-Carter
3 Scarlett Johansson
4 Jennifer Lawrence
5 John Legend
6 Chris Pratt

Cultural note

Dwayne Johnson (born 1972)

Dwayne Johnson, also known as The Rock, is an American WWE wrestler turned movie star. He's been in movies such as *The Scorpion King* (2002) and *The Fast and The Furious* franchise.

Beyoncé Knowles-Carter (born 1981)

Beyoncé is an American singer and actress. Beyoncé, once a member of the group Destiny's Child, is one of the best-selling artists in history. She's married to Jay-Z, the rapper.

Scarlett Johansson (born 1984)

Scarlett Johansson was born in New York. She made her name as an actor in the movie *The Horse Whisperer* (1998). She starred in the movie *Lost in Translation* (2003) opposite Bill Murray.

Jennifer Lawrence (born 1990)

Jennifer Lawrence is an American actor—one of the highest paid in the world. She was the main star of *The Hunger Games* movie franchise and she won an Academy Award for her role in *Silver Linings Playbook* (2012).

John Legend (born 1978)

John Legend is an American singer, songwriter, musician, and actor, best known for his song *All of Me*. He has won ten Grammy Awards.

Chris Pratt (born 1979)

Chris Pratt is an American actor who first came to national attention with a role on the TV comedy *Parks and Recreation* (2009–2015). He's also starred in many movies, including *Guardians of the Galaxy* (2014) and *Jurassic World* (2015).

Life Skills: Studying (SB page 14)

Materials

1

Focus the students on the pictures. Check that they know the English name for each item and have them repeat the words. Ask them to choose 3 of the items for studying English—there may be more items they can use, so they should choose the 3 most important to them. Ask confident students to read out their list and give reasons on why they chose the items they did.

2

Tell students that they can choose one more item—they may have been inspired by some of the choices made by students in Exercise 1.

3 Pairwork

Have students tell their partner their choices, and then discuss their choices using full sentences. Circulate and help any students who are struggling.

Vocabulary Extra (SB page 15)

Everyday objects

1

- Focus the students' attention on the list of words and point out that they're all to do with everyday objects. Point out that the underlining indicates the syllable of the word that has the strongest stress. Check that the students can pronounce all of the words correctly.
- Ask the students to look at the pictures and match each one with one of the words. Point out that the first one has been done for them.

ANSWERS:

6 a bag
8 a book
2 a camera
7 a cell phone
1 a computer
3 a dictionary
5 a key
9 a passport
4 a pen

2 Pairwork

- Demonstrate the activity with a confident student. Begin by asking the question in the example and eliciting the answer. Then get the student to ask you a question about one of the other objects in Exercise 1.
- The students then continue the activity in pairs. Go around, giving help and encouragement, and check that they're pronouncing the words correctly.

Numbers

Ask the students to work individually to match the number figures with the words. Allow them to compare answers in pairs.

ANSWERS:

1 one
2 two
3 three
4 four
5 five
6 six
7 seven
8 eight
9 nine
10 ten

2

Demonstrate the activity with a confident student. Tell them that they should write the words for the numbers rather than the figures. Then put the students into pairs to continue the activity. Go around, giving help and encouragement. Make sure each student takes a turn at saying the numbers.

Further Practice Material

Need more classroom practice activities?
Photocopiable resource materials in the Teacher's Presentation Kit / Extra Resources

Need more tests?
Test Generator
Teacher's Presentation kit / Extra Resources / Tests

Need more on important teaching concepts?
Key concepts in *American Inside Out Evolution* pages xix–xxxiv

Need student self-study practice?
Workbook pages 4–6

Need to check what your students can do by the end of this unit?
Self-evaluation checklists on pages xxxvi–xxxviii

2 International *Overview*

Section	Aims	What the students are doing
Vocabulary SB page 16	Names of countries	Listening to introductions of game show contestants and identifying their countries.
Grammar SB page 16	*Be* (simple present)	Asking and answering questions about where people are from.
Grammar SB page 17	Prepositions: *in* and *near*	Listening and underling the correct answers. Completing a sentence about where they are from.
Speaking SB page 17	Fluency practice	Asking people where they are from. Asking about where other students in the class are from.
Vocabulary (1) SB page 18	Nationalities	Matching nationalities with pictures.
Vocabulary (2) SB page 18	Numbers *11* to *19*, and *20* to *199*	Practicing numbers from 11 to 19, and numbers 20 to 199.
Pronunciation SB page 19	Units of currency	Listening and matching signs to units of currency. Listening and circling prices.
Listening SB page 19	Prices	Listening and completing a table with prices.
Grammar SB page 19	*How much ...?*	Reordering jumbled sentences. Asking questions using *How much ...?*
Language for Life SB page 20	Expressions with *How much ...?* (for shopping)	Listening and completing conversations. Listening and repeating expressions. Practicing conversations.
Life Skills SB page 20	Cultural awareness: food & celebrations	Matching foods to the nation of origin. Identifying different festivals from around the world.
Vocabulary Extra SB page 21	Countries and nationalities Numbers	Matching pictures with words. Dictating and writing numbers.
Writing WB page 9	Using question marks and periods. Writing short questions and answers.	

2 International *Teacher's notes*

Warm-up

Play *Hangman* with the students, using the name of a famous person the students will know. (See page xv for instructions.) Encourage the students to pronounce the letters correctly—so if they say /aɪ/ write *I* even if they mean *E*.

Vocabulary (SB page 16)

1 18

- Focus the students' attention on the pictures and the flags beside them. Note that the people shown are contestants in a TV show; they have to sing in order to win *Rock Star Talent*.
- Write *Mexico* on the board and read it out, emphasizing the first syllable. Ask the students to repeat it after you. Make sure that they're all pronouncing it correctly. Then focus their attention on the table and the stress boxes at the top. Repeat the word *Mexico*, explaining that the three stress boxes show it's a three-syllable word, and that the larger box at the beginning shows that this is the syllable that receives most stress.
- Focus the students' attention on the stress boxes at the top of the other columns in the table. Demonstrate how these words should be stressed. You could use a nonsense syllable like *da* to illustrate. So, the second column would be *DAda*, the third *daDA*, the fourth *DA*. Ask students to repeat after you.
- Ask the students to listen to the recording and pay attention to the way the names of the countries in the box are pronounced. Give them a few minutes to write them in the correct columns of the table before playing the recording again for them to check their answers.

ANSWERS:

1 Mexico **2** Germany **3** Chile **4** Japan **5** Brazil **6** Spain

18

And now on Rock Star Talent, please welcome…
Number 1 from Mexico!
Number 2 from Germany!
Number 3 from Chile!
Number 4 from Japan!
Number 5 from Brazil!
Number 6 from Spain!

Language note

Pronunciation: stress

You can check the stress of any word by looking in your dictionary. Dictionaries usually mark the stress of a word as well as giving the phonetic script, i.e. *Brazil* /ˈbrɒzil/. In this textbook the stressed syllable is always underlined.

Note that geographical names and nationalities are often listed at the back of dictionaries rather than appearing alphabetically in the body of the book.

2 19

- Ask the students to listen and repeat all the country words. Begin with choral repetition, then ask individual students to say the words. Check that their intonation is correct each time.
- Finally, ask what the name of their country is in English. If your class has students from different nationalities, encourage them to pronounce every country represented clearly for everyone to hear.

Grammar (SB page 16)

be

1 20

- A table of the simple present of the verb *be* is shown in the box with both full and contracted forms. Tell the students that in speech you usually use the contracted forms. However, point out that in short answers you say *Yes, I am*, *Yes, he is*, etc., NOT ~~*Yes, I'm*~~ or ~~*Yes, he's*~~.
- Tell the students to look at the information in the box and use it to complete the questions and answers. Allow them to work in pairs if they wish. Go around monitoring and giving help where necessary.

When the students have finished, play the recording for them to check their answers. Then play it again for them to repeat after the speakers.

ANSWERS:

a Is Monika from Germany?
Yes, she is. No, she isn't.
b Is Rosa from Japan?
Yes, she is. No, she isn't.
c Is Victor from Chile?
Yes, he is. No, he isn't.

d	Are Andreas and Ana from Brazil? Yes, they are. No, they aren't.
e	Are you from Spain? Yes, I am. No, I'm not.
f	Are you and your teacher from Mexico? Yes, we are. No, we aren't.

20

a Is Monika from Germany?
Yes, she is.
No, she isn't.
b Is Rosa from Japan?
Yes, she is.
No, she isn't.
c Is Victor from Chile?
Yes, he is.
No, he isn't.
d Are Andreas and Ana from Brazil?
Yes, they are.
No, they aren't.
e Are you from Spain?
Yes, I am.
No, I'm not.
f Are you and your teacher from Mexico?
Yes, we are.
No, we aren't.

Language note

Grammar: contractions–*be*

There are two possible contractions for the negative form of the verb *be* (except for the *I* form where *I'm not* is the only possibility). For example, *you aren't* or *you're not*, *she isn't* or *she's not*.

In the negative, there are two ways of contracting the verb *be*. For example, *No, he isn't* (contracting *not*) or *No, he's not* (contracting *is*). In this textbook only *isn't* and *aren't* are used, but accept both forms from your students as both are correct. Note with *I*, only *No, I'm not* is correct.

Remember that you don't use the contractions in the positive short form answers. You say *Yes, she is*. NOT ~~*Yes, she's*~~.

2

Students work in pairs and take turns to ask each other the questions in Exercise 1. Tell them to base their answers to questions a) to d) on the information given by the flags in Exercise 1. They should give true answers to questions e) and f).

ANSWERS:

a	Yes, she is.	**c**	Yes, he is.
b	No, she isn't.	**d**	No, they aren't.

3 Pairwork

- Put the students in pairs and tell them who will be Student A, and who will be Student B.
- While they're doing the pairwork exercise, go around, monitoring and giving help. Take note of any errors which may need focusing on later and also any examples of good language use which you can praise. Check answers with the class.

ANSWERS:

a Ed Sheeran is from Britain.
b The Kardashians are from the USA.
c Neymar is from Brazil.
d Salma Hayek is from Mexico.
e Angela Merkel is from Germany.
f Jay-Z and Beyoncé are from the USA.

Cultural note

Ed Sheeran (born 1991)

Ed Sheeran is a singer and guitarist from Britain. He has had number one albums in the US and the UK, and has won several Grammy awards.

The Kardashians

The Kardashians are an American family who have become famous through their glamorous lifestyles and the hit reality TV show, *Keeping Up With The Kardashians* (since 2007). The show focuses on the sisters Kim, Khloe, and Kourtney Kardashian and their half-sisters, Kendall and Kylie Jenner.

Neymar (born 1992)

Neymar da Silva Santos Júnior is a Brazilian soccer player who has played for the Brazilian national side and the Barcelona club side. He is one of the world's most popular sports stars.

Salma Hayek (1966)

Salma Hayek is a Mexican actor, star of movies such as *Desperado* (1995) and *Frida* (2002). She has also been the producer of movies and TV shows, including *Ugly Betty* (2006–2010).

Angela Merkel (born 1954)

Angela Merkel is a German politician who became German Chancellor in 2005. She is also the leader of the Christian Democratic Union (CDU) political party.

Jay-Z (born 1969) and Beyoncé (born 1981)

Jay-Z (real name Shawn Carter) is an American rapper who has sold over 100 million records. He is married to Beyoncé, one of the best-selling artists in history.

4 Grammar Extra 2

Ask the students to turn to Grammar Extra 2. Here they'll find an explanation of the grammar they've been studying and further exercises to practice it.

ANSWERS:

1

a I'm from Brazil.
b You're from Mexico.
c He's from Italy.
d She's from Japan.
e They're from Spain.
f We're international!

2

a I'm not from Brazil.
b You aren't from Mexico.
c He isn't from Italy.
d She isn't from Japan.
e They aren't from Spain.
f We aren't international!

3

a Is the Eiffel Tower in Buenos Aires?
b Is Big Ben in New York City?
c Are the Petronas Towers in Cairo?
d Is the Brooklyn Bridge in London?
e Is the Kremlin in Paris?
f Are the Pyramids in the USA?

Grammar (SB page 17)

Prepositions: *in* and *near*

1 21

- Focus the students' attention on the diagrams in the box which show the difference between the prepositions *in* and *near*. Make sure everyone understands these before you move on. Demonstrate by giving an example of places in your country.
- Play the recording and ask them to underline the correct answers. Do the same for b).
- Check answers with the class and then ask the students to work in pairs and take turns to ask and answer the questions.
- Finally, ask them to take turns asking and answering the question *Where are you from?* using true information about themselves. Go around encouraging everyone to use the prepositions correctly.

ANSWERS:

a near; in **b** near; in

21

a Where are you from?
I'm from Paterna. It's near Valencia in Spain.
b Where are you from?
We're from Niteroi. It's near Rio in Brazil.

2

Ask the students to work individually to complete the sentence so it's true for them. Tell students who don't live in a big city to use the word *near* (*I'm from Cuernavaca. It's near Mexico City, in Mexico.*). For students who live in Mexico City, they shouldn't use the word *near* (*I'm from Mexico City. It's in Mexico.*).

Speaking (SB page 17)

1

- Read out the conversation in the speech bubbles to the class. Then choose a confident student and demonstrate the conversation using your own towns, cities, and countries.
- Then ask the students to mingle and ask three other students where they're from.

2

Choose individual students to ask questions about where other students are from. Encourage those who found out the information about these students in the mingling activity in Exercise 1 to answer. Make sure both questions are practiced (*Where is X from?* and *Is X from Y?*).

Vocabulary (1) (SB page 18)

Nationalities

1 22

Focus the students' attention on the flags and nationalities shown in the box. Explain that the words you use for nationalities are always different from the names of the countries. Play the recording and ask the students to repeat the nationalities. When they have done this chorally, ask individual students to pronounce the words.

Language note

Vocabulary: *Britain/England/UK*

People often confuse England and Britain.

England is only one of the three countries that make up Britain. People who come from England are English. Its flag is white with a red cross.

Britain is made up of England, Scotland, and Wales. People from Scotland are Scottish, and people from Wales are Welsh. Each country has a separate flag.

The United Kingdom (the UK) is Britain and Northern Ireland.

Pronunciation: countries

In the word *Chile*, the stress is on the first syllable /ˈtʃɪli/. In the word *Chilean*, the stress can be on the first syllable /ˈtʃɪliən/ or on the second syllable /tʃɪˈliːən/. In this book we use the first option.

In the word *Japan*, the stress is on the second syllable /ja'pɑːn/, and on the third syllable in *Japanese* /ˌdʒæpə'niːz/.

2 ▶ 23

- Ask the students to look at the pictures and see if they can identify any of the people and objects shown. (See Cultural note.)
- Ask the students to work in pairs and decide which description is correct for each picture. When they've finished, allow them to compare notes with another pair before playing the recording for them to check their answers. When they've checked, play it again for them to repeat after the speaker.

ANSWERS:

a	She's British.	**b**	It's Mexican.
c	He's Spanish.	**d**	They're Brazilian.
e	They're German.	**f**	They're Japanese.

Extra activity

To give further practice of *she is/isn't*, ask the class some questions about the pictures. For example, *Is Adele Mexican? Is Javier Bardem from Germany? Are they Mexican?* Get the class to respond chorally.

Get some of the more confident students to ask the class these or similar questions, and get the class to respond. If necessary, give the students time to prepare some written questions about the pictures. This will give you time to help the less confident students. Then get the students to ask and answer these questions in pairs.

Cultural note

Adele (born 1988-picture a)

Adele is an English singer and songwriter. She has sold over 100 million albums, making her one of the century's biggest artists.

Aeroméxico (picture b)

Aeromexico is the largest airline in Mexico.

Javier Bardem (born 1969—picture c)

Javier Bardem is a Spanish actor who has starred in movies such as *Jamón Jamón* (1992) and the Bond movie, *Skyfall* (2012).

Brazilian national soccer team (picture d)

Mercedes-Benz, BMW, and Audi (picture e)

The car badges shown are those of German car companies Mercedes-Benz, BMW, and Audi.

Japanese women (picture f)

The Japanese women in the picture are in the fashionable Shibuya district of Tokyo.

Vocabulary (2) (SB page 18)

1 ▶ 24

Play the recording and ask the students to listen and repeat the numbers. Encourage them to pronounce the ends of all the words clearly, so that they differentiate between numbers that end in *teen* and those that end in *ty*.

Extra activity

To encourage the students to focus on the endings *teen* and *ty* when listening and speaking, tell them that you're going to call out some numbers. If the number ends in *teen*, they should stand up, but if it ends in *ty*, they should remain seated. Call out some different numbers at random. When they understand what to do, ask several students to come to the front of the class and call out numbers for the others to react to.

Language note

Pronunciation: numbers

For some students, it's difficult to differentiate between *teen* and *ty*, for example, in *thirteen* and *thirty*. Point out how the position of the stressed syllable changes.

2 Pairwork

Ask the students to practice saying the numbers 1–20 with a partner.

3 ▶ 25

Ask the students to work individually to complete the lines. Then play the recording for them to check their answers. Point out that when you say numbers over a hundred, it is acceptable to leave out the word *and*, e.g. one *hundred (and) ninety-nine*.

ANSWERS:

a	twenty-three	**b**	thirty-six
c	forty-nine	**d**	one hundred and thirteen

4 ▶ 26

- Explain that the speaker on the recording will tell them which numbers to connect. The first instruction for a) has been followed for them as an example, but note that there's one more instruction to follow for the numbers in a).

- Play the recording, allowing the students time to follow the instructions. When they've connected all the numbers correctly, the lines they've put on the diagrams should spell out a mystery number.
- Ask if anyone can identify the mystery number.

ANSWERS:

The mystery number is TEN.

Pronunciation (SB page 19)

1 27

- Tell students that the symbols in this exercise are symbols for different currencies: the pound sign (£) for the UK, the dollar sign ($) for the United States, Australia, Canada, and several other countries, the Euro (€) sign for most of Europe, the Real sign (R$) for Brazil. Ask the students to match the words and signs and check answers with the class.
- Point out that all the currencies have singular and plural forms: *one pound*, *one dollar*, *one euro*, *one real*. The plural of real is reais.
- Then play the recording and ask the students to repeat the words.

ANSWERS:

a euros = € **c** dollars = $
b pounds = £ **d** real = R$

2 28

- Read the two prices in a) to the class, emphasizing the difference between them. Then play the recording and ask the students to circle the prices they hear. Allow them to compare answers in pairs before checking with the class.

ANSWERS:

a $3.50 **e** €80.20
b £5.30 **f** £40.40
c €70.75 **g** $116.00
d R$19.99

- Play the recording again for the students to listen and repeat.

Listening (SB page 19)

1 29

- Focus the students' attention on the table and the pictures of the different things. Note that all the prices have been put in US dollars for ease of comparison, not because dollars are used in all these cities. Point out that some of the prices in the table are missing and are labeled a) to d). Tell students to listen to the recording and complete the table with the missing prices.
- Play the recording, several times if necessary. Allow the students to compare answers in pairs before checking with the class.

ANSWERS:

a $5.00 **c** $16.50
b $3.50 **d** $210.00

29

a How much is a cappuccino in New York City?
Five dollars.
b How much is a hamburger in Mexico City?
Three fifty.
c How much is a movie ticket in London?
Sixteen dollars and fifty cents.
d How much is a night in a 3-star hotel in Tokyo?
Two hundred and ten dollars.

2 Pairwork

- Ask the student to discuss in pairs how much these things cost in their city, and to complete the table.
- When they've finished, allow them to compare their results with another pair before getting feedback from the whole class.

Grammar (SB page 19)

How much ...?

1 30

- In this section, the students will practice using *How much ...?* to ask questions about prices. Begin by focusing their attention on the example question in the box.
- Ask students to work individually to put the words in the correct order. Check the answers by asking individual students to read out their reordered questions.
- Play the recording for the students to check their answer again, and to repeat the questions after the speakers.

ANSWERS:

a How much is a cappuccino in New York?
b How much is a hamburger in London?
c How much is a movie ticket in Tokyo?
d How much is a night in a 3-star hotel in Mexico City?

2 Pairwork

Ask the students to work in pairs and to take turns to ask and answer the questions. Remind them that the answers are in the table in Listening Exercise 1. Go around, monitoring and giving help.

Language for Life (SB page 20)

1 31

- These short conversations will help students to ask questions about prices of things in stores in the US and Europe. Explain that they don't need to know the words for all the things on sale; they can use *this* and *these*. Remind them that *this* is used for singular things and *these* for plurals.
- Ask the students to work individually to complete the conversations. Then play the recording for them to listen and check their answers.

ANSWERS:

a this
b these
c is
d are

31

a
Man: How much is this?
Woman: It's twenty dollars fifty.
Man: OK, thanks.
b
Boy: How much are these?
Man: Nine dollars.
Boy: OK, thanks.
c
Woman: How much is this?
Woman: Eight euros twenty.
Woman: OK, thanks.
d
Man: How much are these?
Man: One hundred and seventy-five dollars.
Man: Oh! OK, no thanks.

Language note

Grammar: *this/these* or *that/those*

The demonstrative pronouns *that* and *those* aren't taught explicitly in the Beginner level. However, if you feel your students can cope, then this would be a good point to introduce them. In the context of shopping, you can easily demonstrate through mime the concept of using *this/these* for things which are close to the speaker. Then contrast *this/these* with *that/those* for things which are more distant from the speaker.

Vocabulary: *castanets*

Castanets (picture b) are an instrument made up of two pieces of wood tied together by string and knocked together. They are considered plural.

2 32

Play the recording for the students to listen and repeat.

3 Pairwork

- Ask the students to take turns being both the customer and the sales clerk as they practice the conversations. Go around, monitoring and giving help where necessary. Ask a few pairs to perform their conversations for the class.

32

a How much is this?
b How much are these?
c OK, thanks.

Life Skills: Cultural Awareness (SB page 20)

Food and celebrations

1 33

Explain that a big part of cultural awareness is an understanding of how things are different in different countries. In this lesson, we're looking at different foods and celebrations in different cultures. Have students guess the nationality of the food before playing the audio—they aren't expected to know, so this can be turned into a fun game with points for the right answers.

ANSWERS:

a British
b Japanese
c American
d German
e Spanish
f Mexican

Cultural note

Fish & chips

A traditional dish in Britain, the fish is deep-fried in batter, and salt and vinegar is often added to the dish.

Sushi

Sushi is a Japanese dish of vinegared rice with ingredients such as raw fish or vegetables, often wrapped together with seaweed.

Hamburger

A hamburger is a sandwich of a bread bun on either side of a cooked patty of ground meat. It's often served with salad or sauces.

German sausages

There are many different sausages that originate in Germany, such as the bratwurst and frankfurter.

Paella

A Spanish national dish, the paella is a rice dish which comes from Valencia. There are many different versions with different ingredients–meat, seafood, and vegetables.

Taco

A food associated with Mexico, the taco is a wheat or corn tortilla wrapped around a filling like chicken or pork.

2 ▶ 34

Ask students to read the different festivals and try to guess the country before playing the audio to confirm the answers.

ANSWERS:

a Brazil **b** the USA **c** Germany **d** Mexico

3 Pairwork

- Ask the students to play a guessing game using the food and celebrations they have learned about. Go around, monitoring and giving help where necessary. Ask a few confident pairs to perform their guessing games for the class.

Cultural note

Rio Carnival

The Carnival in Rio is a festival held every year before Lent, the period leading up to Easter. The Rio Carnival is the biggest carnival in the world with 2 million people per day on the streets.

Oktoberfest

Oktoberfest takes place in Munich in Germany from mid-September to the first weekend in October. It's probably best known for the large quantities of beer consumed.

Thanksgiving Parade

The Thanksgiving Parade happens on Thanksgiving Day in November and features large inflatable figures.

Day of the Dead

The Day of the Dead is celebrated in Mexico on November 2. This is when the dead are remembered and prayed for. A popular symbol of the festival is the skull.

2 Vocabulary Extra (SB page 21)

Countries and nationalities

1

- Focus the students' attention on the example and establish that *Mexico City* is the name of the city shown in the picture, *Mexico* is the name of the country, and *Mexican* the nationality word.
- Ask the students to look at the other pictures, read the city labels, and to choose the correct words from the box. Go around, giving help and encouragement.
- Point out that the underlining indicates the syllable of the word that has the strongest stress. Ask for choral and individual repetition to check that they are pronouncing all the words correctly.

ANSWERS:

1	**a**	Mexico	**b**	Mexican
2	**a**	Germany	**b**	German
3	**a**	Spain	**b**	Spanish
4	**a**	the USA	**b**	American
5	**a**	Chile	**b**	Chilean
6	**a**	Japan	**b**	Japanese
7	**a**	Brazil	**b**	Brazilian
8	**a**	the UK	**b**	British

Cultural note

The Palace of Fine Arts, Mexico City, Mexico

The Palace of Fine Arts (Palacio de Bellas Artes) is a cultural center in Mexico City. It holds events in music, dance, theatre, opera, and literature.

The Brandenburg Gate, Berlin, Germany

The Brandenburg Gate is a structure in Berlin, Germany. It was built between 1788 and 1791.

The Plaza Mayor, Madrid, Spain

The Plaza Mayor (Main Square) was built during Philip III's reign (1598-1621) and is a central plaza in Madrid.

One World Trade Center, New York, USA

One World Trade Center is a skyscraper located in Lower Manhattan, New York. It was built on the site of the original twin towers of the World Trade Center, destroyed on 9/11.

Plaza de Armas, Santiago, Chile

The Plaza de Armas dates from the 1540s. The area around the Plaza is home to many buildings of cultural and political significance, including museums and the Metropolitan Cathedral.

The Golden Pavilion Temple, Kyoto, Japan

Kinkakuji (the Golden Pavilion Temple) was built in 1397. It's been burned down several times and the present structure dates from 1955. Most of the pavilion is covered with pure gold leaf, and houses relics of the Buddha.

Christ the Redeemer, Rio de Janeiro, Brazil

The statue of Christ the Redeemer stands on the Corcovado hill, which offers stunning views of Rio de Janeiro. At 30 meters tall, it's one of the tallest statues in the world.

Tower Bridge, London, UK

Tower Bridge is a famous bridge across the River Thames in central London. It was built between 1886 and 1894.

Numbers

- Remind the students that in the last unit they matched the words for numbers one to ten with the figures. Ask them to do the same with the numbers from 11 to 100.
- Ask for choral and individual repetition to check that they're pronouncing all the numbers correctly. Pay special attention to the difference between 13 and 30, 14 and 40, etc.

ANSWERS:

11	eleven	**20**	twenty
12	twelve	**30**	thirty
13	thirteen	**40**	forty
14	fourteen	**50**	fifty
15	fifteen	**60**	sixty
16	sixteen	**70**	seventy
17	seventeen	**80**	eighty
18	eighteen	**90**	ninety
19	nineteen	**100**	one hundred

2

Students work in pairs to say the numbers. Demonstrate the activity with a confident student, making sure everyone understands that they have to write the words for the numbers rather than the figures. Go around, giving help and encouragement. Make sure each student takes a turn at saying the numbers.

Writing

Workbook page 9
Using question marks and periods.
Writing short questions and answers.

Further Practice Material

Need more classroom practice activities?
Photocopiable resource materials in the Teacher's Presentation Kit / Extra Resources

Need more tests?
Test Generator
Teacher's Presentation kit / Extra Resources / Tests

Need more on important teaching concepts?
Key concepts in *American Inside Out Evolution* pages xix–xxxiv

Need student self-study practice?
Workbook pages 7–9

Need to check what your students can do by the end of this unit?
Self-evaluation checklists on pages xxxvi–xxxviii

3 Family *Overview*

Section	Aims	What the students are doing
Listening SB page 22	Listening for specific information	Listening to a description of a family and matching names to people. Using family words to complete a family tree.
Grammar SB page 22	*How old …?*	Asking and answering questions about people's age.
Grammar SB page 23	Possessive *'s/s'*	Completing sentences about family relationships. Matching descriptions to names.
Listening SB page 23	Listening for detail	Listening to a conversation and putting pictures in order. Listening and underling the correct word.
Vocabulary SB page 23	Family words	Writing sentences about family relationships.
Reading SB page 24	Reading for detail	Matching descriptions to pictures. Matching people to sentences.
Grammar SB page 24	Possessive determiners	Using possessive determiners to complete sentences.
Grammar SB page 25	*Have* (present simple)	Choosing the correct form of the verb *have*.
Pronunciation SB page 25	Indefinite articles *a* and *an*	Practicing the pronunciation of *a* and *an* in front of nouns. Linking words which end in a consonant with those which begin with a vowel.
Writing SB page 25	Writing a paragraph	Writing a paragraph about a family member.
Language for Life SB page 26	Expressions for introducing people	Listening to a conversation and identifying the people. Listening and repeating expressions for introductions. Writing and practicing introductory conversations.
Life Skills SB page 26	Communication: showing interest	Completing sentences about families. Identify different conversational responses.
Vocabulary Extra SB page 27	Family	Matching pictures with words. Writing sentences about family.

3 Family *Teacher's notes*

Warm-up

Play the game *Secret number* to review the numbers the students learned in Unit 2.

Write a number on the board and get the students to say what it is. Repeat this a few times until the students seem quite confident with numbers.

Then write a number on a piece of paper, hiding the paper in an exaggerated way so that the students can't see the number. Then write a big question mark in the center of the board and ask *What's the number?* Keep pointing at the question mark until one of the more confident students calls out a number. Write the number on the board. Gesture that it's incorrect, and indicate with your hands whether it's higher or lower. If it's more than your secret number, write it above the question mark. If it's less, write the number below.

Encourage the students to suggest other numbers until they find the correct number.

Repeat this game two or three times.

Listening (SB page 22)

1 ▶ **35**

- Focus the students' attention on the illustration. Focus the students' attention on the labels on the image and read them out. Explain that the words used to talk about family members (*Mom, Dad, Grandma, Grandpa*) are informal. The more formal versions are in the list in this exercise, which they have to match to the people's names.
- Read the family words and the list of names, then play the recording and ask the students to match the two.
- Check answers with the class.

ANSWERS:

1 father (dad) = Lucas
2 mother (mom) = Julia
3 brother = Bruno
4 sister = Ana
5 grandmother (grandma) = Maria
6 grandfather (grandpa) = Victor

2 ▶ **36**

Play the recording for the students to repeat the family words from Exercise 1.

3

- Focus the students' attention on the family tree. Remind them of the symbols for male (♂) and female (♀). Point out the key and the explanation that the equals sign (=) means "married to."
- Ask the students to complete the family tree according to the information in Exercise 1.
- Check answers with the class.

ANSWERS:

a Victor	**e** Bruno
b Maria	**f** Luisa
c Lucas	**g** Ana
d Julia	

Extra activity

Ask the students to draw their own family trees.

Ask the students to read the text from the listening activity, and then to write a personal version based on their own family tree.

Grammar (SB page 22)

How old ...?

1 ▶ **37**

- Focus the students' attention on the question and answer in the box. They're going to listen to a girl talking about the ages of the members of her family.
- Play the recording and pause after each question and answer for the students to complete them. Check answers with the class.

ANSWERS:

a How old are you?
I'm six.
b How old is your brother?
He's four.
c How old is your sister?
She's one.

- **d** How old are your mother and father?
  They're forty-two.
- **e** How old is your grandmother?
  She's sixty-eight.
- **f** How old is your grandfather?
  He's seventy.

Language notes

Vocabulary: talking about age

When you talk about your age, you can say *I'm 37* or *I'm 37 years old*. But you can't say ~~*I'm 37 years*~~.

2 Pairwork

Put the students in pairs and ask them to take turns to ask the questions from Exercise 1. Demonstrate first with a confident student. You could teach the sentence *I don't have one*, so that they can answer questions about family members that they don't have.

Extra activity

Ask the students to draw their own family trees if you didn't do the previous Extra activity. Ask the students to add ages to their family tree.

In pairs, the students ask and answer questions about their own family trees.

Grammar (SB page 23)

Possessive *'s/s'*

1 38

- This exercise focuses on the possessive *'s/s'*. Go through the information in the box, making sure everyone understands that *brother's* is singular and *sisters'* is plural. Practice the pronunciation, making sure that the students realize that the possessive *'s* often, but not always, has a */z/* sound.
- Students then work in pairs to complete the sentences. Remind them that the information about Luisa's family is on the previous page.
- Play the recording for the students to check their answers, then play it again for them to repeat.

ANSWERS:

- **a** mother (mom)
- **b** brother
- **c** grandfather (grandpa)
- **d** sister
- **e** father (dad)
- **f** grandmother (grandma)

38

- **a** Julia is Luisa's mother.
- **b** Bruno is Luisa's brother.
- **c** Victor is Luisa's grandfather.
- **d** Ana is Luisa's sister.
- **e** Lucas is Luisa's father.
- **f** Maria is Luisa's grandmother.

Language note

Grammar: possessive *'s/s'*

It isn't usual to say *The house of my brother*. Most native speakers would say *My brother's house*.

To make the possessive form for a singular noun, you add an apostrophe and *s* (e.g. *My friend's brother.*).

The apostrophe *'s* is pronounced like a plural ending (e.g. *teacher's* /ˈtiːtʃərz/, *teachers* /ˈtiːtʃərz/).

If the singular ends in an *s* (e.g. *James*), you usually add an apostrophe after the *s* (e.g. *James' brother*). This is pronounced /ˈdʒeɪmzəz/. It's also possible to write *James's*, which is pronounced the same.

2

Ask the students to work individually to match the names with the descriptions. Then check answers by asking individual students to read out the questions and getting the class to answer them.

ANSWERS:

- **a** Bruno
- **b** Ana
- **c** Julia

Listening (SB page 23)

1 39

- Focus the students' attention on the pictures and tell them that these are pictures from Luisa's family. Explain that they're going to listen to Victor, Luisa's grandfather, talking about these pictures to a friend, and that they have to number the pictures in the order they hear them.
- Play the recording, several times if necessary, and ask the students for the correct order of the pictures.

ANSWERS:

- **1** b Victor and Maria
- **2** a Julia and Lucas
- **3** c Luisa and Ana

39

(V = Victor; F = Friend)
V: This is on vacation in Mexico. This is me, with my wife.
F: Maria?
V: Yes, that's Maria. And this is my daughter getting married.
F: Aah, nice. What's her name?
V: Julia, and her husband's name is Lucas.
F: And are these your grandchildren?
V: This is my granddaughter Ana.
F: How old is she?
V She's one. And this is Luisa. She's six.

2

Play the recording again and ask the students to underline the correct word in each sentence. Check answers with the class.

ANSWERS:

a wife
b daughter
c granddaughter

Vocabulary (SB page 23)

1 40

- Note that some of the family words in the box are used exclusively with male family members, some with female members only, and some with both.
- Play the recording for the students to repeat the words.

2

- Go through the examples with the class and then ask the students to work individually on their six sentences. Go around, monitoring and giving help where necessary.
- Check answers with the class, asking a variety of students to read out their sentences. Ask the other students to look at the family tree, and to check that the sentences which are called out are correct.

3

- The students should work on their sentences individually and then compare them with a partner. Go around the class asking various students to read out one or two of their sentences.

Language note

Vocabulary: additional vocabulary

Students, depending on their family situation, may want to express other relationships not covered by the vocabulary taught. If necessary, give them extra vocabulary, such as *uncle, nephew, niece, stepmother*, etc.

4 Pairwork

- Put the students in pairs and tell them who will be Student A, and who will be Student B.
- While they're doing the pair work exercise, go around monitoring and giving help. Take note of any errors which may need focusing on later and also any examples of good language use which you can praise.

Language note

Vocabulary: further vocabulary

The pairwork exercise introduces a new relationship with the word *boyfriend*. This gives more adventurous students the opportunity to explore further vocabulary in this area. Prepare to give them other words, such as *girlfriend, best friend*, etc.

Reading (SB page 24)

1 41

- Focus the students' attention on the pictures. Do they recognize the people in any of the pictures? Play the recording and ask the students to read the two texts as they listen.

41

a

Hello to the Smiths!
Who's on the red carpet? It's the Smith family!
Fresh Prince of Bel Air actor and movie star, Will Smith, is married to actor Jada Pinkett-Smith.
They have two children. And their children are stars now!
Jaden Smith is an actor and singer, and he was in the movies *Karate Kid* and *After Earth*.
Jaden has a little sister Willow. She is young, but she has a hit song already, with *Whip My Hair*.
Will's eldest son Trey, from his first marriage, is a DJ in Los Angeles.

b

It's a Cyrus family event. That is the Cyrus family
Father, Billy Ray Cyrus, a famous singer, enjoyed the evening with his wife, Leticia.
Billy and Leticia have three children.
Miley Cyrus, is a big TV and music star, and her sister, Noah, is also a pop singer.

Language note

Vocabulary: *actor*

The term *actor* can be used for both men and women. The term *actress* for a female actor does exist, but today actor is more commonly used.

Cultural note

Will Smith (born 1968)

Will Smith is an American actor, producer, rapper, and songwriter. He came to prominence as the rapper The Fresh Prince and starred in the subsequent hit TV series, *The Fresh Prince of Bel-Air (1990-1996)*. He then transitioned to movies such as *Independence Day* (1996) and the *Men in Black* movies (1997-2012).

Miley Cyrus (born 1992)

Miley Cyrus is an American singer, songwriter, and actress. She started out as a child actor in minor TV roles and then became the teen star of the Disney series *Hannah Montana* (2006-2011). She has also had several number one albums in the US, featuring hits like *See You Again* (2007) and *Wrecking Ball* (2013).

2

Go through the sentences and the people with the class. Then ask the students to work in pairs to match them. Check answers with the class.

ANSWERS:

1 d
2 b
3 c
4 a

Grammar (SB page 24)

Possessive determiners

1 42

- Go through the information on possessive determiners in the box. Then read the example sentence with the class. Ask the students to complete the remaining sentences.
- Play the recording for students to check their answers. Play it a second time for them to repeat the sentences.

ANSWERS:

a her
b his
c their
d My; Our
e her; her

42

a Jaden Pinkett-Smith and her daughter are actors.
b Billy Ray Cyrus and his daughters are singers.
c Jaden, Willow, and their parents are all famous stars.
d Miley Cyrus says, "My sister and I are now singers. Our parents are so proud!"
e Noah Cyrus is happy to be a singer like her sister and her father.

Language note

Grammar: review possessive determiners

In the phrase *Billy Ray Cyrus and his wife*, you use *his* because you're referring back to Billy Ray Cyrus.

In the phrase *Letitia Cyrus and her daughters*, you use the word *her* because you're referring back to Letitia Cyrus.

The gender of *his* and *her* depends upon the person you're referring back to and not the person being described.

2 Grammar Extra 3

Ask the students to turn to Grammar Extra 3. Here they'll find an explanation of the grammar they've been studying and further exercises to practice it.

ANSWERS:

1
1 my **2** your **3** he **4** it **5** our **6** their

2
a parents'
b mother's
c father's
d sisters'
e sisters'

Grammar (SB page 25)

have

1 43

- Focus the students' attention on the example sentence. Ask them to work individually to choose and underline the correct form in each sentence.

- Play the recording for the students to check their answers. Play it a second time for them to repeat the sentences.

ANSWERS:

a have
b have
c has
d have
e have
f has

43

a I have one brother.
b My parents have a dog.
c My mother has three brothers.
d My grandparents have two houses.
e My husband and I have two children.
f My father has a Japanese car.

2 Pairwork

Ask the students to discuss in pairs which sentences are true for them, and then to report back to the class.

Pronunciation (SB page 25)

1 44

- Ask the students to listen carefully to the recording. Note the red links between *an* and words beginning with a vowel sound. Explain that all nouns beginning with vowel sounds require *an*, not *a*, as the indefinite article. Demonstrate that this facilitates the pronunciation by comparing how difficult it is to pronounce *a actor* /ə ˈæk.tɚ/ with how easy it is to say *an actor* /ən ˈæk.tɚ/. You might want to note that a word beginning with a vowel doesn't necessarily mean a vowel sound, i.e. *university* /juniˈvɜsəti/.
- Play the recording again and ask the students to repeat the sentences, paying particular attention to the linked words.

2 45

- Focus the students' attention on the table. Remind them that you use the indefinite article *a* before words that begin with a consonant sound and *an* before those that begin with a vowel sound. Read out the example word in each column, being sure to link *an Oreo cookie*.
- Ask the students to put all the words from the box in the correct columns of the table. Encourage them to read the words aloud as they do this, linking any that begin with vowel sounds. Make sure they understand the meaning of all the items in the box.
- Play the recording for them to check their answers, then play it again for them to repeat. Encourage them to link words correctly.

ANSWERS:

an + vowel sound: an Oreo cookie, an English dictionary, an Android cell phone, an Apple computer, an American grandmother

a + consonant sound: a brother, a dog, a Gucci bag, a passport, a sister

3 Pairwork

Give the students a minute or two to think of their own possessions. Give help with any vocabulary they need. Then ask them to take turns to tell their partner about the things they have. Go around, monitoring and giving help where necessary. Encourage them to link words correctly.

Writing (SB page 25)

Extra activity

This writing activity can be quite complex for some students. You could do a "bridge activity" to prepare them for the writing.

On the board, write these sentences:
I have a brother. His name is John. He's 23.
(You can replace the model sentence with true information about yourself if you wish.)

Get some of the stronger students to make similar sentences about themselves. Ask all the students to write three similar sentences about themselves. Then ask the students to go round the class saying their sentences to each other.

1

- This is a simple writing exercise to get the students started on writing short texts. Read the example with the class so that they get an idea of the sort of text they should produce. They can use this example as a model if they wish, but emphasize that they can choose any family member to write about, and can include any details they wish.
- Allow plenty of time for the students to write their short text. As they do this, go around giving help with vocabulary, and checking that the students are constructing their sentences correctly.

2 Pairwork

- Ask the students to read each other's texts. Then encourage them to ask questions about each other's relatives to find out any information that's missing.
- You could elicit the sort of questions they might ask first and put them on the board (*How old is he/she? What is her daughter's name?* etc.).

Language for Life (SB page 26)

1 ▶ 46

- Focus attention on the picture and give the students time to look at it. Tell them that the conversations are taking place at a party.
- Play the recording and ask the students to read the conversations as they listen.
- When they've finished, ask students for their answers to the two questions. Don't confirm whether they're correct or not. Then play the recording again for the students to check.
- Note that *Nice to meet you* is a polite response to an introduction and is short for *It's nice to meet you*.
- Ask a couple of pairs of students to role-play the conversations.

ANSWERS:

a Tim
b Rob

▶ 46

Tim: This is Anna. She's my sister.
Gerry: Nice to meet you. I'm Gerry.
Anna: Nice to meet you.

Rob: This is Sophia. She's Brazilian.
Becky: Nice to meet you. I'm Rob's wife.
Sophia: Nice to meet you.

Language note

Grammar: general review of apostrophe *'s*

The apostrophe *'s* can be confusing for students as it's used for different purposes:

- Contraction of is, for example, *He's Mexican. Where's Wally?*
- The possessive form, for example, *Anna's brother. Becky's husband.*

Point out to students that it's the same form used for different meanings.

2 ▶ 47

Play the recording for the students to listen to and repeat the sentences.

3 ▶ 48

- Ask the students to look at the illustration and the conversation next to it. Ask them to complete the conversation, using the words in the box.
- Play the recording for them to check their answers. Then ask a couple of groups of students to perform the conversation for the class.

ANSWERS:

1 This
2 Nice
3 meet
4 'm
5 to
6 you

4 Groupwork

- Put the students in groups of three and ask them to rewrite the conversation from Exercise 3, using their own names.
- Students should then practice the conversation. Invite confident groups to perform the conversations to the class.

Life Skills: Communication (SB page 26)

Showing interest

1 ▶ 49

Focus the students on the photos as they listen to the conversations for the first time. Then play the audio again, making sure students focus on the responses. Then give students a chance to try and complete the conversations using the words in the box.

▶ 49

a
Anna: Who's this?
Bridget: This is my grandmother, Anna. She's ninety-three.
Anna: Really?
Bridget: Yes. She looks amazing, doesn't she?
b
Luis: And who's this?
Fran: Oh, this is my sister, Esther. She's a doctor at the city hospital.
Luis: Is that right?
Fran: Yes. She's very smart!
c
Shen: Who's this in the photo?
Jenny: He's my grandfather, Ben. He's seventy-two. And he runs marathons.
Shen: No way!
Jenny: I know. We all think he's crazy...
d
Pippa: And who's the boy?
Tom: Ah, that's my son, Will.
Pippa: Where is he?
Tom: He's at his grandparents.
Pippa: Oh, I see.

ANSWERS:

a Really
b right
c way
d see

2 ▶ **50**

Explain that we use these responses to show the talker that we are interested. Role-play with a student a normal response (*I see.*), and then the same conversation with a strong and enthusiastic response (*That's amazing!*). Once students have understood the difference, read the responses and have students repeat. Students should then answer. Play the audio to check their answers.

ANSWERS:

a N
b S
c N
d S
e S
f N
g S

3 Pairwork

In pairs, have students practice the responses. Invite a few groups to perform the conversations to the class.

3 Vocabulary Extra (SB page 27)

Family

1

- Focus the students' attention on the list of words and point out that they're all to do with family. Remind the students that the underlining indicates the syllable of the word that has the strongest stress. Check that the students can pronounce all of the words correctly.
- Ask them to tell each other the names of the brothers, granddaughters, etc., as appropriate.
- Ask the students to look at the pictures and complete the sentences with the correct words from the box.

ANSWERS:

1 husband
2 parents
3 granddaughter
4 brother
5 mother
6 grandfather

2

Ask the students to look at the family tree and answer the questions. You could ask the questions around the class, or perhaps get individual students to ask the questions and to choose another student to answer.

ANSWERS:

a Karl
b Linda
c Fran
d Gary
e Alice and Bill
f Fran

3

Ask the students to write sentences about their families.

Further Practice Material

Need more classroom practice activities?
Photocopiable resource materials in the Teacher's Presentation Kit / Extra Resources

Need more tests?
Test Generator
Teacher's Presentation kit / Extra Resources / Tests

Need more on important teaching concepts?
Key concepts in *American Inside Out Evolution* pages xix–xxxiv

Need student self-study practice?
Workbook pages 10–12

Need to check what your students can do by the end of this unit?
Self-evaluation checklists on pages xxxvi–xxxviii

Review A *Teacher's notes*

These exercises act as a check of the grammar and vocabulary that the students have learned in the introductory unit and the first three units of the Student's Book. Use them to find any problems that students are having, or anything that they haven't understood and which will need further work.

Grammar (SB page 28)

Remind the students of the grammar explanations they read and the exercises they did in the Grammar Extra on pages 58 and 59 of the Student's Book.

1

This exercise reviews language from Units 1, 2, and 3.

ANSWERS:

a What's your mother's name?
b How old is she?
c Where is she from?
d What's her nationality?
e What's her telephone number?
f Where is she now?

a My mother's name is ...
b She's ... years old.
c She's from ...
d She's ...
e Her telephone number is ...
f She's in/at ... now.

2

This exercise reviews *this* and *these* from Unit 1.

ANSWERS:

a What's this?
It's a car.
b What are these?
They're planes.
c What are these?
They're buses.
d What's this?
It's a cell phone.
e What's this?
It's a camera.
f What are these?
They're dictionaries.

3

This exercise reviews the simple present forms of the verb *be*, and nationality words from Unit 2.

ANSWERS:

a It's German.
b They're Mexican.
c They're American.
d It's Japanese.
e It's Japanese.
f They're English.

4

This exercise reviews possessive determiners and family words from Unit 3.

ANSWERS:

a my
b Our
c Her
d Their
e His
f your

5

This exercise reviews possessive *'s/s'* and family words from Unit 3.

ANSWERS:

a wife's
b mother's
c father's
d sons'
e sister's
f brothers'

6

This exercise reviews structures used in Units 1, 2, and 3.

ANSWERS:

1 a) ~~My name Tom.~~
2 a) ~~What is?~~
3 a) ~~Where Mario from?~~
4 b) ~~They're from in Mexico.~~
5 b) ~~I have twenty years.~~
6 b) ~~She have two children.~~

Vocabulary (SB page 29)

1

This exercise reviews classroom language from the introductory unit.

> **ANSWERS:**
>
> **a** Listen
> **b** Practice
> **c** Ask
> **d** Look
> **e** Match

2

This crossword reviews numbers 1 to 10 from Unit 1.

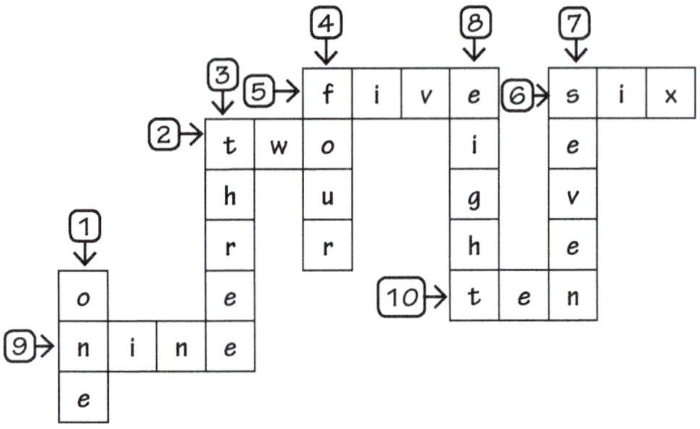

3

This exercise reviews the names of countries from Unit 2.

> **ANSWERS:**
>
> **a** Chile
> **b** Japan
> **c** Spain
> **d** Mexico
> **e** Brazil

4

This exercises reviews units of currency and prices from Unit 2. Remind the students of the different symbols for different currencies.

> **ANSWERS:**
>
> **a** Twelve dollars and fifty-five cents
> **b** Twenty-four pounds ninety-nine
> **c** Fifteen euros seventy-five
> **d** Thirty-seven real eighty

5

This exercise reviews family words from Unit 3. Point out to the students that to complete each pair, they need the equivalent family word, but of the opposite gender.

> **ANSWERS:**
>
> **a** daughter
> **b** mother
> **c** wife
> **d** sister
> **e** son
> **f** father
> **g** husband
> **h** grandmother
> **i** brother
> **j** grandson

Pronunciation (SB page 29)

These two exercises review work students did on word stress, using words they met in Units 1–3.

1

Remind the students of the use of large and small stress boxes to help them get their intonation right. Here they're being asked to classify words according to how many syllables they have and where the main stress falls. Encourage them to say each word aloud to get a feeling for what sounds right.

> **ANSWERS:**
>
> (See Exercise 2 for answers)

2 ▶ 51

Point out the main stresses in the example words, which are underlined. Ask the students to do the same for the other words in the table. Play the recording for them to check their answers.

ANSWERS:

1 and 2

A:	B:	C:
adjective	computer	Japanese
Mexico	description	seventeen
granddaughter	possessive	
singular	Chilean	

Reading & Listening (SB page 30)

1

- You could ask the students to read the sentences first so that they know what information they're looking for when they read the text.
- When you've checked their answers, ask them to correct the false information.

ANSWERS:

a False. (It's in San Francisco.)
b True.
c False. (It has a hundred and twenty rooms.)
d True.
e True.

2 52

- Go through the choices with the students before they listen to the recording so that they know what information they're listening for. You may need to play the recording several times to allow them to find the answers.

ANSWERS:

a 1
b 2
c 3

52

(R = Receptionist; PE = Paula Espinoza)
R: Good afternoon, ma'am.
PE: Good afternoon. How much is one night at this hotel?
R: One night is $190.
PE: Oh, OK. One night, please.
R: Sure, What's your first name?
PE: Paula.
R: Can you spell that?
PE: P-A-U-L-A.
R: And your last name?
PE: Espinoza.
R: Espinoza? Can you spell that, please?
PE: E-S-P-I-N-O-Z-A.
R: Sorry, can you repeat that?
PE: E-S-P-I-N-O-Z-A.
R: Thank you. Do you have a telephone number?
PE: Yes, it's 55-5130-5872.
R: Are from the USA, Ms. Espinoza?
PE: No, I'm not. I'm Mexican. I'm from Mexico City.
R: Your passport number, please Ms. Espinoza?
PE: It's G489-798-23
R: Sorry, can you repeat that, please?
PE: It's G489-798-23
R: Thank you. Here's your key. Your room number is 48.

3

Go through the form with the class so that they can see what information is missing. Then play the recording again so that they can complete it. You may need to play it several times.

ANSWERS:

FIRST NAME:	Paula
LAST NAME:	Espinoza
NATIONALITY:	Mexican
CITY:	Mexico City
COUNTRY:	Mexico
TELEPHONE NUMBER:	55-5130-5872
PASSPORT NUMBER:	G489-798-23

Writing & Speaking (SB page 31)

1

Ask the students to look at the West Side Hotel form. Explain what a capital letter is, and ask them to look at the form and use it to find examples for the rules on the use of capital letters.

ANSWERS:

a Susan
b Barclay
c British
d Wellington Street
e London
f United Kingdom

2

Go through the questions with the class. You could do an example with them first before asking them to match the questions to the numbered information on the form. Check answers with the class before the students work in pairs to ask each other the questions and complete the form with their partner's answers.

ANSWERS:

a 3
b 2
c 5
d 4
e 6
f 1
g 7

Further Practice Material

Need more classroom practice activities?
Photocopiable resource materials in the Teacher's Presentation Kit / Extra Resources

Need more tests?
Test Generator
Teacher's Presentation kit / Extra Resources / Tests

Need more on important teaching concepts?
Key concepts in *American Inside Out Evolution* pages xix–xxxiv

Need to check what your students can do by the end of this unit?
Self-evaluation checklists on pages xxxvi–xxxviii

Before the next lesson

For the Quick review activity in Unit 4, cut out some pictures from magazines of famous people the students will know.

4 Life *Overview*

Section	Aims	What the students are doing
Reading SB page 32	Reading for specific information	Reading and completing a questionnaire on life expectancy.
Vocabulary SB page 32	Common verbs	Completing verb phrases. Making sentences about lifestyles.
Grammar SB page 32	Simple present: *I, you, we, they*	Completing questions and answers about lifestyles. Putting questions in the correct order. Asking and answering questions.
Vocabulary SB page 33	Jobs	Matching jobs with pictures. Matching sentences with jobs.
Listening SB page 33	Listening for detail	Matching people to real jobs and dream jobs. Asking and answering questions.
Vocabulary SB page 33	Days of the week	Listening to and practicing the days of the week.
Vocabulary SB page 34	Daily routines	Listening to and repeating verb phrases for daily routines. Putting verb phrases in order.
Reading SB page 34	Reading for main ideas	Answering questions about a text on a DJ's day. Completing the text with the correct verbs. Marking sentences true or false.
Grammar SB page 35	Simple present: *He, she, it*	Completing questions and answers. Asking and answering questions.
Pronunciation SB page 35	Verbs with extra syllables	Listening to and repeating verbs.
Listening SB page 35	Listening for specific information	Completing times in different time zones.
Grammar SB page 35	Telling the time	Completing a table with times. Writing times in different ways.
Language for Life SB page 36	Expressions for greeting	Listening to and practicing telephone conversations. Listening to and repeating expressions. Completing and practicing a conversation.
Life Skills SB page 36	Time management: my day	Completing a daily schedule. Discussing changes to a schedule.
Vocabulary Extra SB page 37	Jobs The day	Matching pictures with words.
Writing WB page 15	Building a description of a daily routine from notes.	

4 Life *Teacher's notes*

Quick review

This is a quick review of some of the language the students have learned so far. Cut out and bring into class some pictures from magazines of famous people they'll know. Ask the students questions about these people such as:

What's his/her name?
Can you spell that?
How old is he/she?
Where is he/she from?
Do you like (name)?

Give a photograph to some of the more confident students. Get the students to mingle, with the more confident students asking the above questions.

Reading (SB page 32)

1

- Explain life expectancy (the age that a person can expect to reach before they die) and that this may differ according to your gender, your lifestyle, the country you live in, and a variety of other factors.
- Then ask the students, working individually, to read the questionnaire and complete it. Help with any difficult vocabulary.
- Focus the students' attention on the *How to score* section and ask them to calculate their own scores, and then look at the results section.

2 Pairwork

Ask the students to compare their scores with a partner and to look at the answers they each gave to the questionnaire. Note that higher points were awarded in the questionnaire not only for healthier lifestyles (not smoking, getting plenty of sleep, eating healthy food), but also for leading a contented life (liking your job). Genetics also plays a big role: those with old people in their family score much more highly than people whose family members generally die young, and women have an inbuilt natural advantage over men when it comes to longevity.

Vocabulary (SB page 32)

1 53

- Explain that some English verbs are often used in conjunction with other words, producing verb phrases. Check that the students understand the meaning of all the verbs in this exercise, then ask them to match them with the words that they go with. Allow them to work in pairs or compare their results with a partner.
- Play the recording for the students to check their answers. Then play it a second time for them to repeat the sentences.

ANSWERS:

a live
b have
c work
d like
e speak
f eat

53

a I live in an old house. I live with my parents.
b I have one brother. I have an old car.
c I work in an office. I work for Apple.
d I like swimming.
e I speak English. I speak Japanese.
f I eat meat. I eat vegetables.

2

Ask the students to work individually to write six sentences about themselves. They should use the verbs from Exercise 1.

Grammar (SB page 32)

Simple present: *I, you, we, they*

1 54

- Focus the students' attention on the information about the simple present of the verb *speak* in the box. Point out the affirmative and negative forms, the question form, and the short answers. Remind them that the affirmative short answer is *Yes, I do*, NOT ~~*Yes, I speak*~~.
- Ask them to complete the short answers in the exercise. Play the recording for them to check their answers. Play it a second time for them to repeat.

ANSWERS:

a Do you speak Chinese?
Yes, I do. No, I don't.
b Do you smoke?
Yes, I do. No, I don't.
c Do you and your family live in a city?
Yes, we do. No, we don't.
d Do your friends like soccer?
Yes, they do. No, they don't.

e Do you eat meat?
Yes, I do. No, I don't.
f Do your parents have a dog?
Yes, they do. No, they don't.

Extra activity

To give further practice of *do* questions, ask the students to make new questions using the vocabulary in Vocabulary Exercise 1 on page 32.

2 ▶ 55

- Go through the example with the class, then ask the students to put the words in the correct order in the other questions.
- Play the recording for them to check their answers, then play it a second time for them to repeat.

ANSWERS:

a Where do you live?
b Where do you work?
c What languages do you speak?
d What food do you like?
e What music do you like?
f What sports do you like?

3 Pairwork

Ask the students to work in pairs and to take turns asking and answering the questions. Ask them to report back to the class what their partner said.

Language notes

Grammar: *Wh* questions

Notice that the grammar section is limited to questions beginning with *Where* and *What* with *do you*. This pattern or word order is fundamental to question forms in English, but this is the first time the students are exposed to it. It's a good idea to draw a table on the board emphasizing the word order:

Where		*live/work?*
What (food)	*do you*	*like?*
What (language)		*speak?*

Vocabulary (SB page 33)

1 ▶ 56

- Give the students time to look at the pictures and identify the jobs. Then go through the sentences about jobs in the box. Point out the use of the indefinite article with jobs. Ask the students to match them with the pictures.
- Play the recording for them to check their answers. Then play it a second time for them to repeat.

ANSWERS:

a He's a lawyer.
b He's a taxi driver.
c He's a soccer player.
d She's a pilot.
e She's an artist.
f He's a musician.

2 ▶ 57

Ask the students to look at the pictures as they listen to the recording, and to repeat the sentences after the speakers. Focus their attention on the underlining, which tells them which syllables are stressed. Encourage them to pronounce *journalist* /ˈdʒɜːnəlɪst/ correctly.

Extra activity

If your students have jobs, find out what they are and if they know the English words for them.

3 Pairwork

- Put the students in pairs and tell them who will be Student A, and who will be Student B.
- While they're doing the exercise, go around, monitoring and giving help. Take note of any errors which may need focusing on later, and also any examples of good language use which you can praise. Check answers with the class.

SUGGESTED ANSWERS:

Student A
a I'm a sales clerk. I work in a store.
b I'm a journalist. I interview people.
c I'm a soccer player. I play soccer for Mexico.

Student B:
a I'm a doctor. I work in a hospital.
b I'm a farmer. I work outside.
c I'm a taxi driver. I drive taxis.

Listening (SB page 33)

1 ▶ 58

- Explain the difference between a real job (the job you actually do) and a dream job (the job you'd ideally like to do). Focus the students' attention on the pictures and explain that these five people were asked what their real jobs are and what their dream jobs are. The students will listen to interviews and put the number of the person next to their real job and their dream job.

- Play the first interview and point out that this one has been done for them. The interviewee is a teacher whose dream job is a musician.
- Play the recording, pausing after each interview for the students to make their choices and put the numbers in the boxes.
- Check answers with the class, then play the recording again. Point out that only one of the interviewees is actually doing his dream job (the actor).

ANSWERS:

1 teacher; musician
2 lawyer; soccer player
3 taxi driver; pilot
4 student; DJ
5 actor; actor

58

(I = Interviewer; M = Man; W = Woman)

1
I: Excuse me. What do you do?
W: I'm a teacher.
I: What's your dream job?
W: Oh, um, musician.
I: Thank you.

2
I: Excuse me. What do you do?
M: I'm a lawyer.
I: And what's your dream job?
M: My dream job? Soccer player.
I: Thank you.

3
I: Excuse me. What do you do?
M: I'm a taxi driver.
I: What's your dream job?
M: Um, pilot. Yes, pilot.
I: Thank you.

4
I: Excuse me. What do you do?
W: I'm a student.
I: What's your dream job?
W: Oh, I don't know. Um, doctor. No, DJ. No, doctor.
I: Doctor?
W: No, DJ.
I: DJ?
W: Yes, DJ.
I: Thank you.

5
I: Excuse me. What do you do?
M: I'm an actor.
I: What's your dream job?
M: My dream job? Actor!
I: Thank you.

Language note

Vocabulary: *DJ*

A *DJ* /diːdʒeɪ/ is the abbreviation for *disc jockey*, who is a person who plays music on the radio or in clubs. It's more common to say *DJ* and not *disc jockey*.

2 Pairwork

- Read out the conversation in the speech bubbles to the class. Then choose a confident student and demonstrate the conversation using your own jobs and dream jobs.
- Then ask the students to mingle and ask three other students what they do and what their dream job is.

Vocabulary (SB page 33)

Days of the week

1 **59**

Focus the students' attention on the days of the week in the box. Play the recording and ask them to repeat the names of the days after the speaker. Point out the pronunciation of *Wednesday* /ˈwɛnzdeɪ/ and make sure that the students don't try to pronounce the *d* in the middle.

Language note

Vocabulary: days of the week

You always start the days of the week with a capital letter in English.

Some students have difficulty differentiating between Tuesday and Thursday. Point out the pronunciation of /t/ in *Tuesday* and /θ/ in *Thursday*. If necessary, give an exaggerated demonstration of how the tongue is behind the teeth in /t/ and well in front of them with /θ/.

2 Pairwork

Put the students in pairs and ask them to take turns to ask and answer the questions. Demonstrate first with a confident student.

Vocabulary (SB page 34)

1 **60**

Focus students' attention on the pictures. Tell them that the illustrations show the kinds of things people do every day: their daily routine. Give the students time to identify the different actions and read the captions. Then play the recording and ask them to listen and repeat the verb phrases.

2

Give students time to look at the pictures and the verb phrases again, and to decide in which order they happen. Ask them to number the pictures from 1 to 8: 1 for the action that happens first, 2 for the next action, etc.

SUGGESTED ANSWERS:

a	1	**e**	7
b	8	**f**	3
c	2	**g**	5
d	4	**h**	6

Reading (SB page 34)

1 61

Ask the students to look at the picture and then read and listen to the posts about DJ Luiz, ignoring the gaps for now. Play the recording. Ask the students to answer the questions. Check answers with the class.

ANSWERS:

a He works in a recording studio and in clubs.
b His favorite club is Club Liquid in Sao Paulo.

61

Hey, fans! Happy Wednesday!
This is my routine during the week. I get up early, have breakfast, and take my son to school. Then I go to the gym – have to stay fit and healthy. After that I go to work in a recording studio. Right now, we're in Sky Studios. It's a beautiful place. After I finish work, I go home and have dinner with my family. We have two young children, River and Lake, so we all go to bed early. Nice!

Hey, guys! Another Saturday night - who wants to have some fun? On Saturdays, I go to bed in the afternoon and then I go to work. I work all night in the club. I love DJing all night! My favorite club is Club Liquid in Sao Paulo, but I work in clubs all around the world. Visit my website www.djluiz.com for club dates. I work hard, but I also have a good time. So, who's ready for a BIG night?

2

Point out that the verbs that complete the text are *get*, *go*, and *have*. Ask the students to decide which one to put in which gap. Play the recording again for them to check their answers.

ANSWERS:

Post 1
1 get
2 go
3 go
4 get
5 have
6 go

Post 2
7 go
8 have

3

Ask the students to go back over the text to find out if the sentences are true or false. Check answers with the class and ask them to correct the false sentences.

ANSWERS:

a True.
b True.
c False. He goes to bed in the afternoon on Saturdays.
d False. He goes to a club on Saturdays.
e True.

Grammar (SB page 35)

Simple present: *he, she, it*

1 62

- Focus the students' attention on the information in the box about the use of the simple present with *he*, *she*, and *it*.
- Read the question and answers in a) with the class, and then ask the students to complete the other questions and answers.
- Play the recording for them to check their answers, then play it a second time for them to repeat after the speakers.

ANSWERS:

a Does he go to the gym on weekdays?
Yes, he does. No, he doesn't.
b Does he have children?
Yes, he does. No, he doesn't.
c Does he go to bed in the evening on Saturdays?
Yes, he does. No, he doesn't.
d Does he work in clubs all around the world?
Yes, he does. No, he doesn't.
e Does he like his job?
Yes, he does. No, he doesn't.

Language note

Grammar: third person *s*

Studies of native speakers show that the third person *s* is one of the last items of language to be assimilated correctly by some young native speaker learners.

Some of your students may need a great deal of practice before they can produce this form without error.

Note that the omission of the third persons rarely leads to a breakdown of communication.

2 Pairwork

The students take turns to ask and answer the questions in Exercise 1, basing their answers on the information about DJ Luiz in the text on page 34.

ANSWERS:

a Yes, he does.
b Yes, he does.
c No, he doesn't. (He goes to bed in the afternoon.)
d Yes, he does.
e Yes, he does.

3 Grammar Extra 4

Ask the students to tum to Grammar Extra 4. Here they'll find an explanation of the grammar they've been studying and further exercises to practice it.

ANSWERS:

1
a I don't speak Chinese.
b He doesn't smoke.
c I don't drink beer.
d She doesn't have a car.
e I don't live with my parents.
f We don't work in the city.
g It doesn't play music.
h They don't listen to music.

2
a does
b finishes
c gets
d goes
e has
f likes
g studies
h watches

3
"I get up at 4:30 a.m. I go to work at 5:30 a.m. and I finish work at about 1:00 p.m. I get home at 2:00 p.m. and have lunch at 3:00 p.m. I go to the gym in the afternoon. I have dinner at 7:00 p.m. and I go to bed at about 9:30 p.m."

Pronunciation (SB page 35)

1 63

- Focus the students' attention on the table and point out the difference between the verbs in the first column and those in the second. Play the recording and ask the students just to listen to the pronunciation of the verbs. Ask them to notice the extra syllable in the verbs in column B.
- Play the recording a second time for the students to repeat. Encourage them to pronounce the extra syllable in the column B verbs.

Listening (SB page 35)

1 64

- Give the students a couple of minutes to study the clocks. Focus their attention on the explanation of *a.m.* and *p.m.* Point out that *noon* means 12:00 p.m. and teach *midnight* (12:00 a.m.). Ask various students to read out the names of the cities that are labeled.
- Play the recording and ask the students to complete a) to f) with the correct times for the different cities. Allow them to compare their answers in pairs before checking answers with the class, and playing the recording once more for a final check. Encourage them to use *a.m.* and *p.m.* correctly.

ANSWERS:

a San Francisco: 4:00 a.m.
b Buenos Aires: 8:00 a.m.
c London: 12:00 p.m.
d Moscow: 3:00 p.m.
e Hong Kong: 8:00 p.m.
f Wellington: 12:00 a.m.

Language note

Vocabulary: the 24-hour clock

The 24-hour clock is used for talking about travel times.

It's quite acceptable to say that you're catching a plane at 14:30 (pronounced as *fourteen thirty*), but you'd arrange a meeting with a friend for that same time at *two thirty*.

Grammar (SB page 35)

The time

1 65

- Focus the students' attention on the information in the box. Point out the question and the use of *after* as in a *quarter after*, and *to* as in a *quarter to*.
- Remind the students of the meaning of *a.m.* and *p.m.* and explain that you can say *in the morning* instead of *a.m.*, and *in the afternoon* or *in the evening* instead of *p.m.*
- Go through the example with the class and then ask them to complete the table.
- Play the recording for them to check their answers, then play it a second time for them to repeat the times after the speaker.

ANSWERS:

a It's four o'clock in the morning.
b It's eight o'clock in the morning.
c 12:00 p.m.
d It's three o'clock in the afternoon.
e It's eight o'clock in the evening.
f 12:00 a.m.

2 66

- Focus the students' attention on the illustrations of clock displays and point out that these are digital rather than analogue clocks. Explain that there's another way to talk about times without using after or to. Go through a) and b) with the class, explaining that *two twenty-five* and *twenty-five after two* are both ways of saying the same thing; the same with *seven fifty* and *ten to eight*.
- Ask the students to work in pairs to complete the times. Allow them to compare their answers with another pair before playing the recording for them to check.
- Play the recording a second time for the students to repeat all the times.

ANSWERS:

a It's twenty-five after two.
b It's seven fifty.
c It's three thirty-five.
d It's ten fifteen. / It's a quarter after ten.
e It's five-oh-five. / It's five after five.
f It's twelve forty-five. / It's a quarter to one.

Language for Life (SB page 36)

1 67

- Focus the students' attention on the illustration for a few moments before you tell them what's happening: someone has made an international telephone call, forgetting that the person he's calling is in a different time zone. Play the recording and ask the students to read the conversation as they listen. Then elicit the answers to the questions.
- Students should then practice the conversation. Invite confident groups to perform the conversations to the class.

ANSWERS:

a It's 8:30 a.m. in New York.
b It's 11:30 p.m. in Sydney.

67

(Mr. E = Mr. Edwards; J = John)
Mr. E: Hello.
J: Good morning! Is this Mr. Edwards?
Mr. E: Who is this?
J: It's John from New York.
Mr. E: What time is it in New York, John?
J: It's 8:30 in the morning.
Mr. E: Oh. Do you know what time it is in Sydney, John?
J: Er, no. What time is it in Sydney, Mr. Edwards?
Mr. E: It's 11:30 ... p.m.
J: Oh, good evening, Mr. Edwards.
Mr. E: Goodnight, John.

2 68

- Ask the students why they think Mr. Edwards responds to John's *Good evening* with *Goodnight* in the recording in Exercise 1. (He's ending the phone call—*Goodnight* is a way of saying *Goodbye*—and emphasizing the fact that it's night time, and too late for John to be calling him.)
- Play the recording for the students to listen and repeat the phrases.

3 Pairwork

Focus students' attention on the illustration, and ask them to write a similar telephone conversation using the conversation in Exercise 1 as a model. Go around, monitoring and giving help where necessary. When they've finished, ask them to practice their conversation, taking turns to be Ms. Harper and Jenny. Take note of a few good conversations to be performed for the class.

Life Skills: Time Management (SB page 36)

My day

1

Check that students know what a *schedule* is. Ask questions about what students do in the morning, afternoon, and evening. Then have students focus on the diary page, and complete a schedule for a typical day at work or at study.

2 Pairwork

Put students into pairs and have them discuss how they can find more time in their day for studying English. Go around, monitoring and giving help where necessary. Ask students to tell the class about their ideas.

3

Students should re-write their schedule based on their discussions in Exercise 2.

3 Vocabulary Extra (SB page 37)

Jobs

1

- Focus the students' attention on the list of words and point out that they're all to do with the jobs. Remind the students that the underlining indicates the syllable of the word that has the strongest stress. Check that the students can pronounce all of the words correctly.
- Ask the students to look at the pictures and match each one with one of the jobs.

ANSWERS:

4 a doctor
11 a sales clerk
6 a flight attendant
1 an actor
13 a soccer player
3 a DJ
10 a pilot
5 a farmer
12 a secretary
7 a journalist
8 a lawyer
9 a musician
2 an artist
14 a taxi driver
15 a teacher

2 Pairwork

Demonstrate the activity with a confident student. Point to one of the pictures and ask *What does he do?* Elicit the answer. Then put the students into pairs to continue the activity. Go around, checking that everyone is pronouncing the words correctly.

The day

1

- Focus the students' attention on the list of words and point out that they're all to do with the times of day. Remind the students that the underlining indicates the syllable of the word that has the strongest stress. Check that the students can pronounce all of the words correctly.
- Ask the students to look at the pictures and match each one with one of the times of day.

ANSWERS:

3 morning
4 afternoon
2 midnight
6 noon
1 evening
5 night

2

- Ask the students to look at the activities and match each one with one of the times of day.

Writing

Workbook page 15
Building a description of a daily routine from notes.

Further Practice Material

Need more classroom practice activities?
Photocopiable resource materials in the Teacher's Presentation Kit / Extra Resources

Need more tests?
Test Generator
Teacher's Presentation kit / Extra Resources / Tests

Need more on important teaching concepts?
Key concepts in *American Inside Out Evolution* pages xix–xxxiv

Need student self-study practice?
Workbook pages 13–15

Need to check what your students can do by the end of this unit?
Self-evaluation checklists on pages xxxvi–xxxviii

5 Places *Overview*

Section	Aims	What the students are doing
Vocabulary SB page 38	Places and features of cities	Matching pictures with places in New York City. Listing famous places in their own city or country.
Reading SB page 39	Reading for specific information	Reading what three people say about living in New York. Matching people with descriptions. Completing descriptions with *in* and *near*.
Writing SB page 39	Writing a description	Writing a description of where they live and work. Identifying descriptions.
Reading SB page 40	Reading for detail	Choosing one thing to do in New York from a web page. Completing sentences about things to do in a city.
Grammar SB page 40	*There is* and *there are*	Completing information about Central Park. Writing sentences about home cities.
Pronunciation SB page 41	Chants	Listening to and practicing chants using *there is* and *there are*. Writing and practicing new chants with *there is* and there are.
Grammar SB page 41	*Is there?* and *Are there?*	Completing questions and answers. Asking and answering questions. Completing a table.
Language for Life SB page 42	Phrases which are useful when asking about locations	Listening to two tourists in New York. Completing conversations. Listening to and repeating useful phrases for asking directions. Writing and practicing conversations.
Life Skills SB page 42	Decision-making: where to live?	Completing a post about neighborhoods. Discussing the best neighborhoods.
Vocabulary Extra SB page 43	Town and country	Matching pictures with words.

5 Places *Teacher's notes*

Quick review

Ask the students if they know what *NYC* stands for *(New York City)*. Ask them if they know of any other cities that are referred to by their initials. They may be able to name Los Angeles (LA), Washington, DC (DC), and Kuala Lumpur (KL).

Vocabulary (SB page 38)

1 69

- Give the students plenty of time to look at the pictures. Allow them to do the matching activity in pairs and to compare the results with another pair before you play the recording for them to check their answers.
- Play the recording a second time for them to repeat the names. Encourage them to pronounce the /dʒ/ sound in *bridge* correctly. Point out that the sound at the beginner of Chrysler is /k/ rather than /tʃ/. Encourage them to pronounce *museum* correctly as /mjuˈzi.əm/ and *statue* as /ˈstæ.tʃuː/ Point out that ending *-tion* in *station* is pronounced /ʃən/. Also highlight the /l/ sound in *building*. When the students have repeated the names chorally, ask for individual repetition to make sure they're pronouncing them correctly.

ANSWERS:

1 The Chrysler Building
2 Grand Central Terminal
3 Central Park
4 The Statue of Liberty
5 Times Square
6 The Metropolitan Museum
7 Brooklyn Bridge

Cultural note

The Chrysler Building

The Chrysler Building was built in 1930 for the Chrysler car company. It's 1,046 feet high and was, until the construction of the Empire State Building, the tallest building in the world. It's still the world's tallest brick building.

Grand Central Terminal

Grand Central Terminal is the largest train station in the world. It has 44 platforms serving 56 train tracks. It contains restaurants, fast-food outlets, newsstands, a food market, part of the New York Transit Museum, and over forty stores.

Central Park

Central Park is an 843-acre public park in the middle of New York City. It was created in 1857. There are several artificial lakes, two ice-skating rinks, a sports arena, and several children's playgrounds. It's popular with joggers, cyclists, and rollerbladers.

Times Square

Times Square is full of brightly-lit advertising, hoardings, theaters, nightclubs, and bars.

The Metropolitan Museum of Art

The Metropolitan Museum of Art, situated just off Central Park, is the largest art museum in New York City. It has a huge permanent collection of modern and classical works of art from all over the world, and has special exhibitions throughout the year.

Brooklyn Bridge

Brooklyn Bridge crosses the East River from Brooklyn to Lower Manhattan. It's nearly 2,000 meters in length, and at the time of its completion in 1883, it was the longest suspension bridge in the world.

The Statue of Liberty

The statue was a gift to the people of America from France to commemorate the centennial of the United States. It was completed in Paris in 1884 and stands on Liberty Island, at the mouth of the Hudson River in New York Harbor.

2

Ask the students to work in pairs to draw up a list of famous places that they know of in New York. As a whole class, find out how many places have been listed. The following are some suggestions of places in New York: JFK airport, the Guggenheim Museum, Trump Tower, Fifth Avenue, Greenwich Village, Yankee Stadium, Bloomingdales, and Tiffany's.

3 70

- Play the recording for the students to repeat the words. Ask for individual pronunciation of the words afterwards to check that the students have the correct pronunciation.
- Ask the students to find examples in the pictures. When checking answers, encourage them to use the formula set out in the example speech bubbles. (*There's a ... in picture 6*).

SUGGESTED ANSWERS:

There's a building in picture 1.
There's a station in picture 2.
There's a park / a lake in picture 3.
There are buildings in picture 3.
There's a statue in picture 4.
There's a square in picture 5.
There are buildings in picture 5.
There's a museum in picture 6.
There's a bridge / a river in picture 7.

4

Ask the students to work on their own and make a list of famous places in their city or country. Tell students they'll be using the lists for pairwork in the next exercise. Go around, giving help and encouragement.

5 Pairwork

The students take turns to say the name of one of the famous places on their lists. The other student has to say what it is. Go through the examples with the class first, so that they're clear about what they have to do.

Reading (SB page 39)

1 71

- Focus attention on the pictures of the three people and explain that they're all people who live in the Brooklyn neighborhood in New York City.
- Ask the students to read the descriptions as they listen to the recording. For now, all they have to do is match the descriptions to the people. You may need to play the recording more than once. Check answers with the class.

ANSWERS:

a Rick
b Betty
c Sam

71

a
My name's Rick.
I love Brooklyn.
I live in an old apartment in Williamsburg, near the river.
I work in an office near the Williamsburg Bridge.
There are so many great places in Williamsburg – rooftop bars, cool movie theaters, and funky shops.
There is a great atmosphere.

b
I'm Betty.
I love New York and I love Brooklyn.
I live in a modern apartment in the Dumbo area of Brooklyn, near the Brooklyn Bridge.
My office is near my apartment so there is no need to commute.
Dumbo is new but it's growing fast.
There is a great bookstore near my office – great for a visit at lunchtime.
There is also a ferry stop in Dumbo to travel up the river.

c
My name's Sam
I love New York. I live in a brownstone in the center of Prospect Heights.
I work in an art gallery near the Brooklyn Public Library.
There are many cool things to do in Prospect Heights.
There are museums, and there is a great park to relax in.
There is also the Brooklyn Nets basketball arena.

Cultural note

Williamsburg

Williamsburg is a neighborhood in the New York City borough of Brooklyn that has become well-known for its artistic inhabitants, especially writers and rock bands.

Dumbo

Dumbo (/ˈdʌmboʊ/)–short for Down Under the Manhattan Bridge Overpass–is a neighborhood in Brooklyn. Given its proximity to Manhattan and access to the famous Brooklyn Bridge, it has become the most expensive neighborhood in Brooklyn and is home to many tech start-ups.

Prospect Heights

Prospect Heights is a neighborhood in the northwest of Brooklyn, New York City. It is a small yet culturally diverse neighborhood, and is home to museums and parks. The Barclays Center, home to basketball's Nets and hockey's Islanders, was built in this neighborhood.

2

- Remind students of the prepositions *in* and *near* from Unit 2. Ask them to turn back to page 17 for a reminder.
- Give them some time to complete descriptions b) and c) with either *in* or *near*. Check answers with the class.

ANSWERS:

Description b
1 in
2 in
3 near
4 near
5 near
6 in

Description c
1 in
2 in
3 in
4 near
5 in

Writing (SB Page 39)

1

Focus the students' attention on the example and explain that they can use the texts in the previous section as a model. Tell them to write their descriptions on a blank sheet of paper and remind them that they mustn't put their names on their texts. Set a time limit for them to write and, as they do so, go around, giving help and encouragement.

2

Collect the students' descriptions and shuffle them. Then distribute them around the class. Ask the students to read the description they've received, and to try to work out who wrote it. Choose students to read out the texts that they've received, and to say who they think wrote them. The people they name should then say whether or not they're correct.

Reading (SB page 40)

1

- Focus the students' attention on the smartphone screen and give them plenty of time to familiarize themselves with it. Tell them that it's an app advertising things to do in New York City. Ask the students to read the text silently to themselves.
- Ask each student to choose the best thing to do in New York City. Then put them in pairs or small groups to compare their choices. Then, as a whole class, find out what the top attraction was.

Extra activity

In Vocabulary Exercise 2 on page 38, the students named other famous places in New York. Ask them to write more things to do in New York, following the pattern in the reading text. For example, *Go to the top of the Statue of Liberty. Go down Broadway. Go to the Guggenheim Museum.*

2

Ask students to complete the sentences using places from a city in their own country.

Language note

Vocabulary: *go down/up, go out*

- The verb *go* combines with many particles to form some of the most common phrasal and prepositional verbs. These are so frequently used in English that it's a good idea to start introducing them to students at this early stage.
- To *go down* a street has the idea of going from a higher place to a lower one (Uptown and Downtown in Manhattan get their names because Uptown is on a hill.) If you walk in the opposite direction, *you go up* the street.
- To *go out* here means to spend an evening outside the home with some form of entertainment, for example, at a restaurant, a movie theater, or a bar. You can use it to invite someone to do something with you, for example, *Do you want to go out on Saturday night?*

Cultural note

One World Trade Center

One World Trade Center is new skyscraper in Lower Manhattan, New York City. It is part of the rebuilt World Trade Center that was destroyed on 9/11. It's height in feet is 1.776, which represents 1776, the year of the USA's independence. There is an observatory on floors 100–102.

High Line

The High Line is a 1.45 mile-long park on the west side of Manhattan. It was created from an old elevated railroad, and gives users views of different neighborhoods and the Hudson River. It gets busy—there are 5 million visitors annually.

Brooklyn Bridge

Brooklyn Bridge crosses the East River from Brooklyn to Lower Manhattan. It's nearly 2,000 meters in length, and at the time of its completion in 1883, it was the longest suspension bridge in the world.

Tribeca

Tribeca (/traɪˈbɛkə/) is a neighborhood in Lower Manhattan—the name comes from the description "Triangle Below Canal Street". It has become New York's safest and most expensive neighborhoods and is home to stars such as Jay-Z, Taylor Swift, and Robert De Niro.

9/11 Memorial Museum

The 9/11 Memorial Museum commemorates the attacks on September 11, 2001 which brought down the twin towers of the World Trade Center and killed nearly 3,000 people. It is located on the site of the buildings, and the underground museum includes artifacts, videos, and photos of the attacks and rescue efforts.

Grammar (SB page 40)

there is / there are

1 72

- Point out the information about *there is* and *there are* in the box, and ask the students to look back at the text on this page and underline all the examples of *there is* and *there are*. Point out that *there is* is used with singular nouns and *there are* with plurals.
- Ask the students to complete the information about Central Park.
- Play the recording for them to check their answers, then play it a second time for them to repeat the sentences.

72

a There's a zoo.
b There are 36 bridges.
c There are three restaurants.
d There are six cafés.
e There's a museum.
f There are 25 million visitors every year.

2

This could be done for homework. If you choose to do it in class, go around while the students are writing, and help with any individual problems.

Pronunciation (SB page 41)

1 73

- Remind the students of the work they did on linking words previously, when words that end in a consonant link with words that begin with a vowel. Ask them to practice saying *There's a* and *There are*, linking the two words together each time.
- Tell them that they're going to hear the sentences in A and B in a chant. Ask them to listen to the recording and repeat the two chants.

2

Allow the students to work in pairs to write their chants. They should practice saying it aloud in their pairs. Go round and note any particularly good ones which you can ask the students to perform for the class.

Grammar (SB page 41)

Is there ...? / Are there ...?

1 74

- Focus the students' attention on the question forms *Is there ...?* and *Are there ...?* in the box. Check that they can pronounce these questions correctly by asking three students to read the first question and the two answers aloud, and another three to read the second question and the answers. Encourage them to use correct pronunciation.
- Ask the students to work individually to complete the questions and answers.
- Play the recording for them to check their answers. Then play it a second time for them to listen and repeat.

ANSWERS:

a Is there a station near your house? Yes, there is. No, there isn't.
b Are there any restaurants near your house? Yes, there are. No, there aren't.
c Is there a museum in your city? Yes, there is. No, there isn't.
d Is there a park near your house? Yes, there is. No, there isn't.
e Are there any hotels in your city? Yes, there are. No, there aren't.
f Is there a church near your house? Yes, there is. No, there isn't.

2 Pairwork

Put the students in pairs and ask them to take turns asking and answering the questions for themselves.

3 Pairwork

- Put the students in pairs and tell them who will be Student A, and who will be Student B.
- While they're doing the exercise, go around, monitoring and giving help. Take note of any errors which may need focusing on later and also any examples of good language use which you can praise.

4

Go through the words in the box and check that everyone understands them and can pronounce them correctly. Then ask the students to complete the table. They should do this individually and then compare their completed tables with a partner.

Extra activity

Do a chain memorization activity based on *There is/are* and the vocabulary in the table of Exercise 4. Write on the board *There's a beach in my city and ...*, and encourage a confident student to finish the sentence.

Then ask another student to repeat the sentence and add another element.

You will find a full explanation of this technique in the Practical methodology section in the Introduction.

Cultural note

Manhattan

New York City is made up of five boroughs of which Manhattan island is the best known. It's the cultural and financial center of the city, and most of New York's famous sights and buildings can be found here.

5 Grammar Extra 5

Ask the students to turn to Grammar Extra 5. Here they'll find an explanation of the grammar they've been studying and further exercises to practice it.

ANSWERS:

1

a 7 = days in a week
b 26 = letters in the English alphabet
c 60 = minutes in an hour
d 50 = states in the USA
e 24 = hours in a day
f 11 = players on a soccer team

a There are seven days in a week.
b There are twenty-six letters in the English alphabet.
c There are sixty minutes in an hour.
d There are fifty states in the USA.
e There are twenty-four hours in a day.
f There are eleven players on a soccer team.

2

a there are ~~*any*~~ / *some* dictionaries.
b there's *a* / ~~*an*~~ map of the USA.
c there are ~~*any*~~ / *some* Brazilian students.
d there's ~~*a*~~ / *an* old CD player.
e there's *a* / ~~*an*~~ computer.
f there are ~~any~~ / some pictures.

3

a there aren't any dictionaries.
b there isn't a map of the USA.
c there aren't any Brazilian students.
d there isn't an old CD player.
e there isn't a computer.
f there aren't any pictures.

Language note

Grammar: *some/any, a/an*

- In this unit, students are introduced to *there is* and *there are* to talk about things that exist. They learn that *there are* is followed by *some* + a plural noun, and that in questions and negatives, *Are there* and *There aren't* are followed by *any* + a plural noun.
- At this level, it's probably not appropriate to go into any more detail on the uses of *some* and *any*.
- Remind students that using *a* or *an* does not depend on the spelling of the word that follows it, but the pronunciation of the word. In most cases, *an* is used before words that begin with vowels (a, e, i, o, u) and *a* is used before words that begin with consonants. Some examples of words with different pronunciation are *hour* which starts with a vowel sound and *one* which starts with a consonant sound. The correct usage is therefore *an hour* and *a one* (e.g. *a one-man band*).
- Students may come across the phrase *Would you like some …?*. It would appear to contradict the rule that the students have learnt in Unit 5, i.e. that *some* is used in affirmative sentences, *any* in negatives and questions. In fact, *some* is used in situations where the question isn't a real question, but a request or an invitation, and the answer *yes* is expected. Encourage students to learn these as complete phrases.

Language for Life (SB page 42)

1 75

- Focus the students' attention on the pictures and ask them to read out the words in the box and to match them to the pictures.
- Play the recording for them to check their answers. Then play it a second time for them to listen and repeat the words.

ANSWERS:

a a pharmacy
b an ATM (an automated teller machine)
c a subway station
d a restroom

2 75

- Give the students a couple of minutes to look at the illustrations and try to decide what the situation is in each conversation.

- Ask them to read the conversations as they listen to the recording. At this stage all they need to do is to identify what each tourist asks for. Check answers with the class.

> **ANSWERS:**
>
> A pharmacy and a restroom.

3

Ask the students to try to complete the gaps in the conversations without listening to the recording again. Then play it for them to check their answers.

> **ANSWERS:**
>
> **1** there
> **2** near
> **3** pharmacy
> **4** Excuse
> **5** there
> **6** near
> **7** Near

76

> **(M = Man; W = Woman)**
>
> **a**
>
> **M:** Excuse me. Is there a pharmacy near here?
> **W:** A what?
> **M:** A pharmacy.
> **W:** A pharmacy? Er, yes –over there.
> **M:** Thanks.
>
> **b**
>
> **W:** Excuse me. Is there a restroom near here?
> **M:** A restroom?
> **W:** Yes, yes, a restroom.
> **M:** A restroom? Near here? No.
> **W:** Oh!

4 77

- Point out that *Excuse me* is a polite way of attracting someone's attention, particularly when you want to ask them a question.
- Play the recording for the students to repeat the phrases. Then ask them to say the first phrase, substituting a variety of other things in place of pharmacy. For example, *Excuse me, is there a park near here? Excuse me, is there a museum near here?* etc.

Life Skills: Decision-making (SB page 42)

Where to live?

1

Focus the students' attention on the text and explain that it is a comment posted on a website. Ask students what the writer wants (help in deciding on a New York neighborhood).

2

Ask students to look at the three tables—each one is looking at a different neighborhood in New York City, and weighing up their positive and negative aspects. Confirm with students that they understand all the terms.

3

Have students discuss in pairs the different options using full sentences and the structures of *there is* and *there are*. Circulate and help any students who are struggling.

> **Cultural note**
>
> **Park Slope**
>
> Park Slope is a neighborhood in northwest Brooklyn in New York City. It is a desirable neighborhood with great schooling, nightlife, shopping, and access to public transit, and is famous for its brownstone buildings.
>
> **East Village**
>
> East Village is a neighborhood in the New York City borough of Manhattan. It is well known for its diverse community, nightlife, and artistic community.
>
> **Astoria**
>
> Astoria is a neighborhood in the northwestern corner of the New York City borough of Queens. It is on the East River and is a diverse, middle-class neighborhood.

4

Ask a student to read out the structures, completing them with their own ideas. Encourage students to write in the style of a comment on a website. Have pairs of students read their recommendation to the class.

5 Vocabulary Extra (SB page 43)

Town and country

1

- Focus the students' attention on the list of words and point out that they're all to do with the town and country. Remind the students that the underlining indicates the syllable of the word that has the strongest stress. Check that the students can pronounce all of the words correctly.
- Ask the students to look at the pictures and match each one with one of the words. Point out that the first one has been done for them.

ANSWERS:

14 an airport
3 a bar
15 a beach
12 a bridge
5 a church
13 a lake
2 a movie theater
6 a museum
11 a park
7 a restaurant
4 a school
8 a square
10 a station
9 a statue
1 a theater

2 Pairwork

Demonstrate the activity with a confident student. Cover the words, point to one of the pictures, and ask *What's this?* Elicit the answer. Then put the students into pairs to continue the activity. Go around, checking that everyone is pronouncing the words correctly.

Further Practice Material

Need more classroom practice activities?
Photocopiable resource materials in the Teacher's Presentation Kit / Extra Resources

Need more tests?
Test Generator
Teacher's Presentation kit / Extra Resources / Tests

Need more on important teaching concepts?
Key concepts in *American Inside Out Evolution* pages xix–xxxiv

Need student self-study practice?
Workbook pages 16–18

Need to check what your students can do by the end of this unit?
Self-evaluation checklists on pages xxxvi–xxxviii

6 Clothes *Overview*

Section	Aims	What the students are doing
Vocabulary SB page 44	Colors	Matching numbers and colors.
Listening & Vocabulary SB page 44	Listening for specific information Colors and clothes	Completing descriptions of clothes with colors. Listening and matching names to people.
Reading SB page 45	Reading for detail	Reading texts about clothes and matching them to pictures. Completing a table with information from texts.
Grammar SB page 45	Present progressive	Completing questions and answers. Asking and answering questions about clothing.
Pronunciation SB page 46	Intonation with *ing* words	Listening and repeating chants with *ing* verbs. Writing and practicing a chant.
Listening SB page 46	Listening for specific information	Matching pictures and descriptions. Matching people and actions.
Speaking SB page 47	Talking about what you are doing	Completing and practicing conversations.
Vocabulary SB page 47	Verb phrases with *do, play, read, and make*	Completing verb phrases. Practicing using verb phrases.
Grammar SB page 47	*How often ...?* Adverbs of frequency	Put questions into the correct order. Completing sentences with adverbs.
Language for Life SB page 48	Expressions when buying clothes	Listening to a conversation and matching it to a picture. Listening and repeating expressions for buying clothes. Writing and practicing new clothes store conversations.
Life Skills SB page 48	Organization: *How often do you ...?*	Completing a questionnaire Discussing changes.
Vocabulary Extra SB page 49	Colors Clothes	Matching pictures with words.
Writing WB page 21	Posting on Instagram	

6 Clothes *Teacher's notes*

> **Language note**
>
> **Pronunciation: *clothes***
>
> The word *clothes* can be difficult for some students to pronounce. You say /kloʊ(ð)z/. Note also that *clothes* has no singular, instead you can say *something to wear*. For example, *I'm going to buy something to wear to the party.*

Vocabulary (SB page 44)

1 78

- The colors on the recording are in the same order as those on the page so encourage the students to look at these as they listen to and repeat the color words.
- Find out what everyone's favorite color is and which is the most popular color in the class.

2 Pairwork

- Focus the students' attention on the numbers and colors. Demonstrate the activity with a confident student. Read out a number and get the student to say what color it is. Then reverse roles.
- Put the students in pairs to continue the activity. Go around, monitoring and giving help. Encourage the students to pronounce the color words correctly.

3 Pairwork

- This exercise takes the color game one step further. Explain, using the example, that the colored number chart can be used to do simple equations.
- Ask the students to make up some simple sums to ask each other. Make sure they also work out the answers. Then put them in pairs to practice asking and answering math questions.

> **Extra activity**
>
> If your students enjoy this, you could divide them into teams and then call out some more "math" questions for them to answer. Give a point to the team that calls out an answer first.

Listening & Vocabulary (SB page 44)

1 79

- Focus the students' attention on the four fashion models. Go through the colors in the box and ask the students to use them to complete the descriptions of the clothes the models are wearing. Check answers by asking individual students to read out the items. Explain any unknown words and help them with the pronunciation of words like *skirt* /skɝt/, *shirt* /ʃɝt/, and *suit* /sut/.
- Play the recording for the students to listen and check. Then play it a second time for them to repeat.

ANSWERS:

a
1 a black jacket
2 a white T-shirt
3 blue pants
4 black shoes

b
1 a blue hat
2 a green top
3 a gray skirt
4 purple boots

c
1 a red dress
2 black shoes

d
1 a gray suit
2 a blue tie
3 a blue shirt
4 red and white sneakers

> **Language note**
>
> **Vocabulary: *T-shirt / tee shirt***
>
> Some words in English have alternative spelling, as spelling has not been standardized. *T-shirt* is one example. Both *T-shirt* and *tee shirt* are commonly used.
>
> **Vocabulary: *pants*, etc. are plural**
>
> Items of clothing with two legs are plural: *jeans, pajamas, shorts, pants, underpants*. However, you can talk about a (singular) *pair of jeans, a pair of shorts, a pair of pants*, etc.

2 80

Play the recording for the students to match the names of the models with the pictures.

ANSWERS:

Leon = a
Kate = b
Jasmine = c
Jason = d

Reading (SB page 45)

1 81

- Focus the students' attention on the pictures and ask them if they think these are the kinds of clothes these people wear every day. Point out that they probably wear them for special occasions, but not every day.
- Play the recording and ask the students to read the three texts as they listen. You may need to play the recording more than once. Explain any unknown vocabulary.
- Ask the students if they had/have to wear a uniform at school. Find out if any of the students come from a country which has a national costume, and ask them to describe it.

Language note

Vocabulary: *sari*

A sari comes from the Indian subcontinent. It is clothing for a female and consists of a drape up to 8 meters long which is then wrapped around the waist, with one end over the shoulder, and worn like a long dress.

It is often made of cotton or silk, and is worn on more formal occasions likes a wedding.

Vocabulary: *hakama*

A hakama is a traditional Japanese garment that is worn over a kimono. It is tied around the waist and extends down to the ankles. Hakama may be open like a skirt or may have legs like pants and are worn by both men and women at formal occasions, and for martial arts.

Pronunciation: a *uniform*

You use *a* before a consonant sound, even if it starts with a vowel. For example, *a uniform* /ˈjunəfɔɹm/, *a university* /juniˈvɝsəti/. You use *an* before a vowel sound, even if it starts with a consonant. For example, *an hour* /ˈaʊɚ/, *an honor* /ˈɑːnɚ/.

2

Ask the students to work in pairs to complete the table. Go around, giving help and encouragement. Check answers with the class.

ANSWERS:

People
Veena and Sita
Kumiko
Peter and Sam
Job
call center workers
a student
teachers
Clothes they usually wear
white shirts and black skirts
T-shirt and jeans
tracksuits
Clothes in the picture
Indian clothes—silk saris
a hakama
hats, suit jackets, and waistcoats

81

a As a student, Kumiko usually wears a T-shirt and jeans, but today is a special day for Kumiko and her friends. Kumiko is graduating from college, so she's wearing a hakama. This is traditional Japanese clothing that students wear for graduation day.

b Veena and Sita are having fun this weekend in Mumbai, India. It's their friend's wedding, so they are dressing up. Look at those beautiful Indian clothes! They work in a call center. There Veena and Sita usually wear white shirts and black skirts, but today they are dancing at a wedding in beautiful and colorful silk saris.

c Peter and Stan are Physical Education teachers - but not today.
They're going horse racing. Peter and Stan are wearing hats, suit jackets, striped pants, and waistcoats.

Grammar (SB page 45)

Present progressive

1 82

- Focus the students' attention on the information about the present progressive in the box. Ask them to read out the different forms and the example sentences. Then ask them to look back at the texts in the previous section and underline any examples of the present progressive. Tell them that these are used to describe what the people are wearing at the present moment, and that the simple present is used to describe what they usually wear. Go around the class asking individual students what they are wearing. Encourage them to use the present progressive in their replies.
- Focus the students' attention on the questions and answers. Go through the first one or two with the class and then ask them to complete the rest. Monitor and help where necessary.
- Play the recording for the students to check their answers. Then play it a second time for them to repeat.

ANSWERS:

a Are Veena and Sita wearing black skirts?
Yes, they are. No, they aren't.
b Are they dancing?
Yes, they are. No, they aren't.
c Is Peter wearing sneakers?
Yes, he is. No, he isn't.
d Are Veena and Sita having a great time?
Yes, they are. No, they aren't.
e Is Yuko wearing jeans?
Yes, she is. No, she isn't.
f Is she holding a parasol?
Yes, she is. No, she isn't.

Language note

Grammar: simple present versus present progressive

The difference between the simple present and the present progressive can be confusing for students even at an advanced level. However, here the difference is clear. You use the simple present to talk about what you do regularly or every day, and you use the present progressive to talk about what you are doing now.

Further uses and differences will be met at higher levels. For the moment, beginners just need lots of practice of the structure.

2

The students can do this in pairs, taking turns to ask a question and to find the correct answer in the photos. Check answers with the class.

ANSWERS:

a No, they aren't.
b Yes, they are.
c No, he isn't.
d Yes, they are.
e No, she isn't.
f No, she isn't.

Extra activity

Play *Who is it?* Describe what one of the students is wearing. The students have to decide who you are describing.

To make this more fun, start with a description that could apply to several of the students, for example, *This student is wearing jeans. Who is it?* Then give more detail until the students guess who it is.

Then describe other students for the class to guess. Let the more confident students describe what their classmates are wearing, too.

3 Pairwork

- Put the students in pairs and tell them who will be Student A, and who will be Student B.
- While they're doing the exercise, go around, monitoring and giving help. Take note of any errors which may need focusing on later and also any examples of good language use which you can praise. Note any pairs whose work is particularly good, so you can ask them to perform their conversations to the class.

4 Grammar Extra 6

Ask the students to turn to Grammar Extra 6. Here they'll find an explanation of the grammar they've been studying and further exercises to practice it.

ANSWERS:

1
A speak-speaking; do-doing; play-playing
B have-having; make-making; write-writing
C sit-sitting; run-running; get up-getting up

2
A go-going; learn-learning; read-reading; sleep-sleeping; study-studying; work-working
B come-coming; dance-dancing; take-taking
C stop-stopping

3
[students' own answers]

4
a What's she doing? She's running.
b What are they doing? They're dancing.
c What are they doing? They're playing soccer.
d What's he doing? He's reading.

Pronunciation (SB page 46)

1 83

- Point out that the underlining indicates the syllable of the words that is stressed. Point out that in the *ing* verbs, it's the first syllable that is stressed.
- Play the recording and ask the students to repeat the chants. Encourage them to copy the intonation of the speakers.

2

- Point out that the first two questions of the three chants in Exercise 1 involved pairs of verbs with opposite meanings. Go through the pairs of verbs in the box and explain any the students don't know. Then ask them to choose pairs of verbs to create a new chant. They could do this in pairs if they wish. Go around, monitoring and giving help.
- Finally, ask the students to practice their chants, perhaps performing them for the rest of the class.

Listening (SB page 46)

1

- Focus the students' attention on the pictures and establish that each one shows someone who is receiving a phone call from someone else.
- Read out the three descriptions and ask the students to match the descriptions to the pictures.

ANSWERS:

a 2
b 3
c 1

2 84

- Ask the students to look at the pictures in Exercise 1 again. Explain that in each case, the person being telephoned is going to tell the other person what they're doing. However, they aren't going to tell the truth!
- Play the recording. Ask the students to match the pictures (showing what the people are really doing) with the sentences in which they say what they're doing.

ANSWERS:

a 3
b 1
c 2

84

a
(H = Husband; W = Wife)
H: Hello, Kate.
W: Oh, hi, honey.
H: Where are you?
W: Oh, um, I'm at the grocery store.
H: What are you buying for dinner?
W: Er, for dinner? Fish. I'm buying fish for dinner.
b
(L = Liza; D = Don)
L: Hello, Don.
D: Oh, hi, Liza.
L: What are you doing?
D: Er, I'm making dinner.
L: Ah, good.

c
(M = Mother; S = Son)
M: Hello.
S: Hi, Mom.
M: What are you doing?
S: Er, I'm doing my homework?
M: Great.

Speaking (SB page 47)

1 Pairwork

- Focus the students' attention on the first picture and the completed conversation. Ask the students what other things the person could have said in response to the question *Where are you going?*
- Put students in pairs. Ask them to look at the second and third pictures and the conversations and to discuss how to complete them. You could check that they've formed the two questions correctly before they move on to deciding how to answer them.
- Go around, monitoring and giving help. Take note of any particularly interesting or amusing conversations which you can ask the students to perform later.

ANSWERS:

a Where are you going? I'm going to Chicago.
b What are you making? I'm making ...
c What are you listening to? I'm listening to ...

2 Pairwork

In the same pairs, the students practice their conversations. Ask some of them to perform them for the class.

Vocabulary (SB page 47)

1 85

- Remind the students that verb phrases are verbs that are commonly used in conjunction with other words. Ask them to look at a). Read out the phrases *do the housework* and *do the laundry* with the class.
- Read out the other verbs: *play, read,* and *make*. Ask the students to work in pairs and decide which goes in which diagram.
- Play the recording for them to check their answers, then play it a second time for them to repeat the verb phrases.

ANSWERS:

a do
b make
c play
d read

Language note

Vocabulary: *do* versus *make*

Do and *make* are combined with nouns to talk about actions you perform. *Do* is often used when the action is a noun ending in *-ing*. For example, *do the shopping, do the cooking, do some sightseeing*, etc. It's also used to talk about daily activities or jobs. For example, *do homework / housework / the ironing / the dishes / a job*.

Make is often used to talk about an activity that creates something. For example, *make food / tea / a mess*.

However, there are a number of fixed expressions using *do* and *make* that don't fit into these categories. For example, *do business / make your bed*. Encourage the students to learn these as complete phrases.

2

Go through the phrases in the box and ask the students to make more verb phrases with *do, play, read*, or *make*. Allow them to compare results in pairs before you check answers with the class.

ANSWERS:

a make dinner
b play a computer game
c read a newspaper
d do your homework

3

- Demonstrate the activity by choosing one of the activities and miming it in front of the class. Ask a student *What am I doing?* and elicit an answer using the present progressive. For example, *You're doing the housework*.
- Put the students in pairs to continue the activity. Go around, giving help and encouragement.

Grammar (SB page 47)

How often ...?

1

- Point out the question in the box: *How often do you drink coffee?* and the answers. Go around the class asking a number of students the same question, perhaps varying the drink each time. Make sure they understand the difference between *How often?* and *When?* Ask them *When do you drink coffee?*
- Look at the example with the class. The other sentences follow the same pattern, but with different verbs, so they should be quite simple for the students to work out.
- Allow students to compare answers in pairs before checking as a class.

ANSWERS:

a How often do you wear sneakers?
b How often do you do the laundry?
c How often do you wear a hat?

2 Pairwork

Students take turns asking and answering the questions.

Adverbs of frequency

3 86

- Focus the students' attention on the table in the margin showing adverbs of frequency. Point out that these are on a continuum from 0% to 100%. Read the example sentences below and ask for a few more examples from the class, e.g. *I never wear jeans, I sometimes wear a hat*.
- Play the audio. Students choose the correct adverb of frequency.

ANSWERS:

a always
b sometimes
c never
d usually
e usually

Language note

Grammar: adverbs of frequency

Adverbs of frequency come before a main verb: *She always wears sneakers.*

Adverbs of frequency come after *be*: *She's always happy.*

4

- The students should work individually to complete the sentences.
- Put the students in pairs to compare their answers and practice telling each other about their clothing habits. You may like to teach *Me, too* and *Me, neither*, so that students who agree with their partner's statements can have something to say.

Language for Life (SB page 48)

1 87

- Focus the students' attention on the pictures and ask them what type of stores they are: a) a sports store, b) a men's clothes store and c) a women's clothes store. Explain that in each store a customer is deciding what clothes to buy. Then play the recording and ask the students to say which picture matches the conversation.
- Point out some of the useful language demonstrated in the conversation. We often use *I'm looking for (a dress)* when someone asks if they can help. It's gentler and more polite than *I want (a dress)*. Explain *prefer* and make sure the students can pronounce it with the correct intonation /pɹɪˈfɜ˞/.

ANSWERS:

Picture C

87

Sales clerk: Can I help you?
Customer: I'm looking for a dress.
Sales clerk: A dress.
Customer: Yes, a dress.
Sales clerk: What size are you?
Customer: It's for my wife.
Sales clerk: What size is she?
Customer: I think she's medium.
Sales clerk: What color?
Customer: Red.
Sales clerk: Do you like this one?
Customer: How much is it?
Sales clerk: It's $500.
Customer: And how much is the blue dress over there?
Sales clerk: It's $90.
Customer: I prefer the blue dress.

Language note

Grammar: stative verbs *like*, *prefer*, etc.

Some verbs are never or rarely used in the progressive form. Some of the common non-progressive verbs refer to mental or emotional states rather than actions, e.g. *believe, like, prefer, love*. You say *I believe it. (NOT ~~I'm believing it.~~)*

However, in the case of the verb *love*, McDonald's® uses the slogan *I'm lovin' it*, which deliberately plays on the fact that this is non-standard English.

2 88

Play the recording for the students to listen and repeat the expressions. Check that they're copying the intonation of the speakers, and ask for individual repetition of the phrases afterwards.

3 Pairwork

- In pairs, the students write similar conversations for one of the other pictures in Exercise 1. Go around, giving help and encouragement. Give help with any extra vocabulary that they need (for example, they may ask how to describe the stripes on the sneakers).
- When they've finished, ask them to practice their conversations. Select a few pairs to perform theirs for the class. Play the recording for them to check their answers. Then ask a couple of groups of students to perform the conversation for the class.

Life Skills: Organization (SB page 48)

How often do you ...?

1

- Focus the students' attention on the picture of a stressed office worker. Ask students for reasons why he might be so stressed. Elicit that the person is completely disorganized. Make clear that students are going to complete a questionnaire on their own—work through the questions as a class if needed. Students who are not currently in a job can still take the questionnaire, but can adjust it slightly for their situation (e.g. *replace meetings* with *classes*, *workspace* for *study space*, etc.).
- Once students have completed the questionnaire, they should calculate their score and look at the key to see how organized they are. Go around the class asking if people are organized or not.

2 Pairwork

Students work with a partner to look back at the questionnaire and what they could change to become more organized. For example, they could decide to make sure their email inbox is clear by the end of the day.

Extra activity

Students then retake the questionnaire based on the things they have decided to improve. Check with students if they are planning to be more organized in the future.

6 Vocabulary Extra (SB page 49)

Colors

1

- Focus the students' attention on the list of colors. Check that the students can pronounce all of the words correctly.
- Ask them to look at the pictures and match each one with one of the words. Point out that the first one has been done for them.

ANSWERS:

7 purple
6 gray
9 black
5 white
10 pink
4 green
3 yellow
8 orange
11 brown
2 red
1 blue

Clothes

1

- Focus the students' attention on the list of words and point out that they're all to do with clothes. Remind the students that the underlining indicates the syllable of the word that has the strongest stress. Check that the students can pronounce all of the words correctly.
- Ask the students which of the items are worn by men, which by women, and which by both.
- Ask them to look at the pictures and match each one with one of the words. Point out that the first one has been done for them.

ANSWERS:

7 boots
3 a dress
11 a hat
8 a jacket
4 jeans
10 pants
12 a shirt
14 shoes
1 a skirt
2 sneakers
6 a suit
13 a tank top
9 a tie
5 a T-shirt

2 Pairwork

Demonstrate the activity with a confident student. Cover the words, point to one of the pictures and ask *What's this?* Elicit the answer. Then put the students into pairs to continue the activity. Go around, checking that everyone is pronouncing the words correctly and using *It's* and *They're* appropriately.

Writing

Workbook page 21
Posting on Instagram

Further Practice Material

Need more classroom practice activities?
Photocopiable resource materials in the Teacher's Presentation Kit / Extra Resources

Need more tests?
Test Generator
Teacher's Presentation kit / Extra Resources / Tests

Need more on important teaching concepts?
Key concepts in *American Inside Out Evolution* pages xix–xxxiv

Need student self-study practice?
Workbook pages 19–21

Need to check what your students can do by the end of this unit?
Self-evaluation checklists on pages xxxvi–xxxviii

Review B *Teacher's notes*

These exercises act as a check of the grammar and vocabulary that the students have learned in Units 4, 5, and 6 of the Student's Book. Use them to find any problems that students are having, or anything that they haven't understood and which will need further work.

Grammar (SB page 50)

Remind the students of the grammar explanations they read and the exercises they did in the Grammar Extra on pages 60 and 61 of the Student's Book.

1

Focus the students' attention on the example and remind them of the two ways of saying the time that they practiced in Unit 4.

ANSWERS:

1 d
2 c
3 e
4 b
5 a

2

Remind the students of the verbs for daily routines that they studied in Unit 4.

ANSWERS:

1 works
2 gets
3 has
4 goes
5 has
6 works
7 has
8 finishes
9 gets
10 goes

3

This exercise reviews the use of *there is* and *there are* in affirmative and negative statements, and in questions. Make sure that the students contract *there is* to *there's* in speech, but that they understand what the full form is. Remind them that you use *some* in affirmative statements (*There are some nice shops*), but this tends to change to *any* in questions (*Are there any nice shops?*).

ANSWERS:

a There are
b There's
c There's
d There are

a Are there any good restaurants?
b Is there a park?
c Is there a theater?
d Are there any hotels?

4

Check that they've put the adverbs of frequency in the right order.

ANSWERS:

1 always
2 usually
3 sometimes
4 not usually
5 never

5

Point out to the students that you use the present progressive to describe things that are happening at the moment. Ask them to look at the illustration and complete the sentences. Check answers.

ANSWERS:

a is talking
b is drinking
c is reading
d is working
e is eating
f is sleeping

Vocabulary (SB page 51)

1

All these jobs were taught in Unit 4.

> **ANSWERS:**
>
> **a** taxi driver
> **b** doctor
> **c** lawyer
> **d** artist
> **e** journalist
> **f** flight attendant

2

When the students have completed the questions, ask them to work in pairs and take turns asking and answering them.

> **ANSWERS:**
>
> **a** get up
> **b** go to work
> **c** have lunch
> **d** get home

3

Point out that the pictures are clues for the words that fit in the crossword. Allow the students to work in pairs to complete the crossword if they wish.

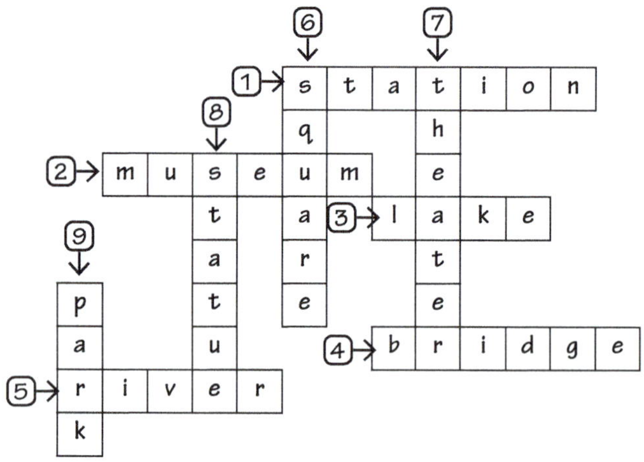

4

Remind the students that they studied color and clothing words in Unit 6.

> **ANSWERS:**
>
> **a** She's wearing a red dress.
> **b** He's wearing black shoes.
> **c** Tom's wearing a blue jacket.
> **d** Maria's wearing a pink skirt.

Pronunciation (SB page 51)

These two exercises review work students did on word stress, using words they met in Units 4-6.

1

Remind the students of the use of large and small stress boxes to help them get their intonation right. Ask individual students to read out the words in the four columns of the table and make sure that they're using the correct stress. Then ask them to add the words from the box to the table. Encourage them to say each word aloud as they do the exercise so that they can get a feeling of what sounds right.

2 89

Ask the students to underline the stressed syllables. They don't need to underline anything in the one-syllable words. When they've finished, play the recording for them to check their answers. Then play it a second time for them to repeat the words.

ANSWERS:

1 and 2

A:	**B:**	**C:**	**D:**
France	jacket	Brazil	museum
jeans	taxi	Madrid	musician
gets	watches	o'clock	relaxes

Reading & Listening (SB page 52)

1 90

Ask the students to read the text as they listen to the recording. Then ask them to underline the correct information. Check answers with the class.

> **ANSWERS:**
>
> **a** 1
> **b** 3
> **c** 3
> **d** 3
> **e** 1

2 91

The conversation isn't printed on the page, so the students will have to listen carefully to get the information they need. You may need to play the recording several times.

ANSWERS:

a True.
b True.
c False. It's one o'clock in the afternoon in London. It's eight o'clock in the morning in New York.
d True.
e True.
f True.

91

(D = Dan Harvey; S = Sosanna)
D: Hello, is this Sosanna?
S: Yes, Sosanna speaking. Who's this?
D: Hi, I'm Dan Harvey. I work for musicexpress.com here in London.
S: Oh, OK What time is it in London?
D: Er, it's one o'clock in the afternoon.
S: Well, Dan, it's eight o'clock in the morning here.
D: Oh...er, sorry, Sosnna. Look, can I ask you some questions for our website?
S: Er, yes, OK.
D: So...where do you live?
S: Here, in New York City.
D: OK. And where do you work?
S: In R&B clubs.
D: OK. What languages do you speak?
S: Er, English ... and Spanish. My husband's Mexican, you know.
D: Oh. Who's your favorite musician?
S: Mavis Staples.
D: Ok, could you spell her last name?
S: Sure, it's Staples. S-T-A-P-L-E-S.
S. She's an R&B and gospel singer.
D: Uh huh. And what's your favorite color?
S: Er, um ... red?
D: What's your favorite city? Do you like London. Or L.A.?
S: Er, yes, I do. But I love New York City!
D: Oh. And what's your favorite food?
S: Pasta.
D: OK. And finally, what time do you usually get up?
S: 11:30.
D: Oh, yes, sorry! Thank you, Sosanna! Goodbye!
S: Have a good day!

3

Go through the information with the class before you play the recording again so that they know what information they're listening for.

ANSWERS:

Name: Sosanna
Lives: New York City
Works: in R&B clubs
Speaks: English and Spanish
Favorite musician: Mavis Staples
Favorite color: red
Favorite city: New York City
Favorite food: pasta

Writing & Speaking (SB page 53)

1

Go through the examples and the rules with the class. Make sure everyone understands the meaning of the plus and minus signs (affirmative and negative statements). Check answers with the class.

ANSWERS:

a
+ / + I play my guitar and I listen to music.
b
+ / - I speak English, but I don't speak Spanish.
- / + I don't have a sister, but I do have a brother.

2

Do the first item as an example with the whole class and then ask the students to do the others. Go around, monitoring and giving help where necessary. Check answers with the class.

ANSWERS:

a I watch TV and I relax.
b She has a computer and she has a camera.
c I speak English but I don't speak Chinese.
d I eat fish but I don't eat meat.
e We get up and we have breakfast.
f I play the piano and I play the guitar.

3

This is a guided writing exercise. The students can use the text about Sosanna on page 52 of the Student's Book as a model. Give help where necessary.

4 Pairwork

Ask the students to look at the form first so that they know what information about their partners they'll have to get. This will help them formulate the correct questions. If your students need extra help, go through the questions they'll need to ask for each piece of information required on the form first with them.

5

This could be set for homework. If you do it in class, go around, giving help where necessary. You could display the profiles on the wall of the classroom for other students to read, or select a few to be read out in class.

Further Practice Material

Need more classroom practice activities?
Photocopiable resource materials in the Teacher's Presentation Kit / Extra Resources

Need more tests?
Test Generator
Teacher's Presentation kit / Extra Resources / Tests

Need more on important teaching concepts?
Key concepts in *American Inside Out Evolution* pages xix–xxxiv

Need to check what your students can do by the end of this unit?
Self-evaluation checklists on pages xxxvi–xxxviii

Notes

Notes

Notes

Notes

Notes

Notes